No Spring Chicken

THOUGHTS ON A LIFE WELL LIVED

No Spring Chicken

THOUGHTS ON A LIFE WELL LIVED

Eileen Comstock

FIFTH
HOUSE

Front cover art by Brian Smith / Articulate Eye
All photos from the author's collection, or those of her family
Design by Articulate Eye

The publisher gratefully acknowledges the support of The Canada Council for the Arts and the Department of Canadian Heritage. We acknowledge the financial support of the Government of Canada through the Book Publishing Industry Development Program for our publishing activities.

THE CANADA COUNCIL | LE CONSEIL DES ARTS
FOR THE ARTS | DU CANADA
SINCE 1957 | DEPUIS 1957

National Library of Canada Cataloguing in Publication Data

Comstock, Eileen, 1926-2001.
No spring chicken

ISBN 1-894856-06-6

1. Comstock, Eileen, 1926-2001. 2. Prairie Provinces–Biography. 3. Prairie Provinces–Humor. I. Title.
FC3243.C65A3 2002 971.2'03'092 C2002-910777-6
F1060.92.C65A3 2002

Printed in Canada by Transcontinental Printers.

02 03 04 05 06/ 5 4 3 2 1

Fifth House Ltd.
A Fitzhenry & Whiteside Company
1511-1800 4 St. SW
Calgary, Alberta, Canada
T2S 2S5
1-800-387-9776
www.fitzhenry.ca

Table of Contents

This book is dedicated to the memory of my wife, Eileen Comstock. Also a special thanks to my son, Keith, and his wife, Janet. Their many hours of hard work on our behalf helped make this book possible.

Evert R. Comstock
July 2002

Foreword

Wife, mother, grandmother, daughter, sister, friend, teacher, farmer, artist, philosopher, historian—and author. Eileen Comstock was all of these people. To me, her son, she was most of all "Mom." In this foreword, I hope to give readers a bit of insight into who she was and how she came to write the stories found within these pages and in her other books. My brother, Lyle, deserves credit for some of the words that follow, as in places I have borrowed from the eulogy we gave jointly at Mom's funeral on 25 July 2001.

Mom was the oldest of the Kopperud children and the only one to be born at home, with her grandmother acting as midwife. From that point on, she never stopped learning, and took that gift with her throughout the rest of her days. When my brother, sister, and I were young we heard the stories of her childhood, first offered as her way of helping us to understand who she was and how things were in her day, and then again as we asked many more times, "Tell us about when you were a kid."

We always had great respect for Mom's knowledge, and as kids felt that she knew everything. Anyone who ever had the misfortune to play Trivial Pursuit against her would probably express the same sentiment. But the game by that name was a latecomer as far as we kids were concerned. Time after time, Mom roped us in to help with dishes with a challenge to play "trivia." She would wash and we would dry, asking and answering questions back and forth about every subject under the sun. About the only thing we could stump her on was sports, as this was not one of her favourite subjects, but there was little else we could get by her. We also learned not to push the sports stuff too far, as then her questions to us would go from difficult to "How the heck would I know?"

Mom loved learning and was a voracious reader. I am nearly certain that the Moose Jaw Public Library's circulation numbers dropped at least a percentage point or two right after her death. As a teacher, Mom had a favorite saying: "There is *no* such thing as a dumb kid—there is only a teacher who hasn't figured out how to get through to them yet." Mom used to say that a good teacher had to have at least five methods for teaching any lesson. I know for a fact that she did, because she needed all five of them for me on more than one occasion. I can recall the joyful look on her face when a student finally "got it"—she truly loved the challenge of helping others.

Although I am not sure she consciously thought about it, I know Mom related very strongly to the oral history tradition, common to Scandinavian and Aboriginal cultures. Depending on the situation, her stories amused, soothed, entertained, inspired, and taught the listener in a way that was sincere and meaningful, but not overly preachy. Although her stories often had a moral or a message, we never felt like that was the most important part; we just liked to hear the words.

When Mom talked about being a storyteller, her advice was to start at the beginning and continue on to the end, without getting lost in the middle. Basic but sage advice that she took to heart in her own writing. Mom also tried very hard to be a good technical writer. She worked at it, studied it, went to workshops and classes, and was an active member of several writing groups over the years.

Perhaps most important was Mom's subject matter. She wrote from her own experience, partly because, as she said, she had "very little creative imagination, but a very good memory," but also because that was what she knew best and felt most strongly about. She saw both the amusing and the ironic in everyday things, and effectively used these viewpoints to get her message across.

Humour, in fact, was a very big part of Mom's writing style. While her stories are not all necessarily "laugh out loud" hilarious, most of them will certainly give you a chuckle or two, as well as the opportunity to reflect on how funny and strange life really is. Those who know the writing craft far better than I describe Mom's humour as "pithy," "tongue-in-cheek," "dry," "wise-cracking," and even occasionally "acerbic." All I know is that every time I read the story about Dad taking out the headlight of the '29 Chev with the crank—on purpose—I laugh!

Our family is very proud of Mom's writing and of her success as an author. In addition to receiving critical acclaim, we have received feedback from all over North America and even from the United Kingdom. Her stories seem to resonate in some way with everyone who reads them—some people enjoy the humour, and others feel the same way as she did about life and family. And for many it seems that the most powerful feeling is that of having shared similar experiences—one person even wrote that it seemed Mom had "lived her life."

Whatever your motivation for reading these stories, I hope you enjoy them. On behalf of my dad, Evert; my brother, Lyle; my sister, Karen; all of our families; and, of course, on behalf of Mom, thanks for reading.

Keith L. Comstock
July 2002

A field of durum wheat awaiting harvest.

※

Prairie Treasure

This prairie holds me in an embrace so strong,
    So knotted, to break it would break me.

Baby leaves uncurl from bare brown twigs.
    Glassy sloughs pasture the sky's sheep.
Packers leave brown twill pattern on fresh seeded fields,
    And a spotted fawn lies unmoving as the tractor circles round.
His aria over, on a grey post the meadow lark bobs and bows
    To sprouting seeds pushing earth teepees up in rows.
Treble peepers sing their nightly chorus,
    And bittern's deep kerchunk, kerchunk plays bass.

A flash of yellow, wild canaries play hide and seek
    With the wild flamenco dance of butterflies.
Fallen old-rose petals carpet a bush of scarlet buds.
    Minty tang of crushed tansy sharp in the nose.
Raw carrots, rubbed clean, still tasting of soil,
    Fresh green peas, nibbled from the pod,
Sweet new potatoes, rosy as baby toes,
    Crisp cucumbers, cool and beaded with secret dew,
Strawberries like hidden rubies under tangled green.
    Eden's garden held no richer fare.

Shooting stars fill August's velvet sky, too many to wish on.

Oceans of ripened grain wave under Aurora's shimmering chiffon.

Waiting on a hilltop for a load of grain, I watch the combines' firefly lights
In all the country round.

Hear my truck's slow powerful rumble as it makes new tracks in the
pale stubble

To fill the silver granaries with hard red wheat and amber durum,
A farmer's silent answer to a hungry world's cry.

A startle of partridge, orange, brown and whirring
Below bow waves of geese, loudly skeining south.

The head-clearing magic of simmering chili sauce,
Crunch of homemade dills with hints of garlic,
And a buttery slab of fresh-baked bread still warm.
Rows of shining jars—jam, jelly, pickles,
Wait on basement shelves, summer's bounty preserved.

The chill sun glints on frost-jewelled trees.

Red fox and tawny coyote trail through drifted fields.
His regal rack bobbing, a stag rounds up his wives,
Takes cover in the bush-thick ravine.

Somewhere, from the trees, the quiet of night is broken by a mournful,
inquisitive owl.

The cold sharp air holds a hint of woodsmoke.
The gold that I treasure is gold of the heart,
The gold of senses and of solitude.
These are my gold pieces, and I—

I am a prairie Croesus.

The Good "Old" Days

BESIDES BEING INEVITABLE, GROWING OLD
CAN ACTUALLY BE FUN!

"Are you a senior?" the clerk asks diffidently. She knows that she treads a fine line. Is this lady going to be offended at the presumption of more years than she has yet acquired, or will she get annoyed at not being offered the senior's discount to which she is entitled? Only a very young, inexperienced clerk can handle this situation with insouciance. To her (usually it is a "her"), anyone older than her parents is old, very old indeed. I never was too upset with that question, because I realized that when I was young, *my* grandmother, who seemed older than mud then, was only in her fifties.

"The Golden Years," "Sunset Homes," "Pioneer Village," "Rest Home," "Geriatric Centre." Don't we pussyfoot around trying to avoid the word "old"? We dance around "old" just as we say "passed on," "at rest," "gone to her reward," "at peace," instead of "dead." Surely at our age we should be able to look simple words in the face. What are we afraid of? "Old" is great!

Just consider what has preceded old age. Childhood, even a good one, is the time when everybody bosses you around. No matter what age a child is, he is too young to do anything he really wants to do, and too old to act the way he really feels—an exercise in frustration. Surely none of us really wants to be a teenager again, when a zit was a calamity, sitting out a dance or two was the height of embarrassment, the guys that seemed interested in you were all nerds, and the ones you liked never noticed you, so you had to pretend you didn't give a hoot.

I remember the days of young parenthood with fondness. It was a busy, happy time. I remember the kids were so cute, and came out with the funniest things. However, after about three days of caring for the grandkids, just as cute and funny as their parents were, I start to remember how there was no end to the cleaning, tidying, picking up, meals, lunches, snacks, fingerprints, laundry, mending, peacemaking, and bedtime battles. And the hauling around—band practice, ball games, football practice, 4-H meetings, music and swimming lessons, inoculations, dentist appointments, and more. The clock was such a tyrant. School bus time, mealtime, practice time, church time. I wouldn't have missed those years for a million dollars. I wouldn't go through them again for two million.

Old is relaxing. I used to rise with the alarm, dress, make breakfast, get the kids up, make school lunches, find four pictures of things that contain vitamin C for the second-grader who forgot about it last night, find matching mittens, fix a zipper, check for grime behind the ears, and arbitrate bathroom time—all before I really woke up. Now, first thing, I sit around in my pyjamas and drink a cup of coffee. Or two. Or three. I am never expected to get all sweaty and mosquito-bitten playing softball at family gatherings. Instead, I can sit on the sidelines and brag about what a great first baseman I used to be before I got bifocals. The only one who can dispute this, my sister Carolie, is too busy explaining how she used to bat home runs before arthritis got her feet.

Old is restful. I had a nap after dinner yesterday, and I will probably have another one tomorrow. If I decide to go to bed and read at eight thirty in the evening, I do. If my dusting isn't done today, next week will do just as well. The best advice a doctor ever gave me was "When you get tired, quit." I guess I needed permission, and I am so glad I got it.

Old is guilt-free. If I get hot under the collar and blow my top, I know I am not going to ruin my children's psyches forever. If the people I care for do dumb things, I no longer wonder what I did that made them so foolish. I just say "That is dumb"—to myself, of course. If I can't remember where I put the bill for the spark plugs, I say "I forget." It usually shows up in somebody else's pocket, anyway. I do not have to be polite to rude old people anymore. (My memory of childhood humiliation is clear enough that I make a point of being polite to youngsters.) For a member of a generation raised on guilt, and one who as a young adult was showered with books and magazine articles that blamed all the ills of society on Momism, or the uncaring community (which I knew also meant me), I have recovered well.

Old is carefree. When I hear a child at a public function howl in pain, frustration, or just plain orneriness, I know it isn't mine. The pocketbook stress that comes with keeping offspring fed, clothed, educated, and amused is now over. Any help we give to the younger generation is given because we want to, not because we have to. We have served our terms in community work and with 4-H and PTA. Our time and money is ours to spend wisely, or fritter away. Frittering is highly underrated, in my opinion.

Old is fun. Old is travel, painting lessons, craft shows, garage sales, crosswords, reading, eating out, visiting, and family history. Old is getting someone else to paint the house while I prune the roses. Brothers and sisters are close again, now that we all have fewer demands on our time. My advice is listened to, now that it has acquired a patina of age and "wisdom." And, if it is not followed, it bothers me not at all.

Old is great! In fact, I have decided that I am going to be old and stay old for the rest of my life.

Prairie blooms in the author's garden.

The Gardening Urge

LOST SEEDS AND LINEN CLOSETS

I didn't have to buy any garden seeds last year. I usually get the gardening urge about the middle of February. When it is cold and windy and I have just about had it with winter, I get out the seed catalogue and for a couple of hours I can imagine myself all warm and earthy, making nice rows and patting down the damp soil. I always think that the best part of travel is looking back on it, rather than actually doing it, and gardening is about the same, but in reverse. Looking forward to gardening is a lot more fun than struggling with weeds, bugs, and rototillers. But I do enjoy it. Of course, I also enjoy complaining about it.

But, as I say, last year I didn't order any seeds. You see, about the end of January the year before, I put the seeds away after they came in the mail. Toward the end of April, I tilled the garden, raked it, and came into the house to get the seeds, but they weren't there. I looked on the shelves downstairs, in the porch closet, in the "everything closet," in the kitchen cupboards, in the garden shed, and in the spare dresser drawers. No seeds. Nowhere.

My husband, Ev, and daughter, Karen, both suggested more places to look. I looked. I told Karen that maybe I just wouldn't plant anything. She said, "I believe you. Hundreds wouldn't, but I believe you!" A little sarcasm there, I thought, but of course she was right. I went to town and bought a whole new batch of seeds.

Years ago I planted great big gardens, with rows about thirty inches apart. My husband used to suggest that after

I rototilled it all up, I might as well start rototilling the summerfallow, seeing I was going so great. After we got a good well and could water the garden, I decided to break a small plot close to the well in the backyard, plant rows close together, and have a "city garden." And that is what I did—almost. I put quite a few potatoes down in the summer-fallow field, near the dugout. Corn plants are hard to pull out in the fall, so they went there, too, so Ev could whack them out with the cultivator. Also, because I have rheumatic knees and like to pick peas and beans sitting between wide rows, I planted them down near the dugout as well.

Our backyard, where the well is and the little garden used to be, is surrounded by lilacs and Siberian elms. The elms soon caught on that the garden was nice and moist, and they sent their roots to visit. I learned that it doesn't pay to fight with Siberian elms. So I broke up another plot or two, far from those intruders, and I am gradually getting grass back into the first plot.

So the year before last, as I was saying, I planted the second set of seeds, and things just popped up. I had nearly forgotten about the first seeds, when, sometime in July, Ev discovered the still unopened parcel in the linen closet. Whoever heard of anyone putting seeds in the linen closet? The whole neighbourhood enjoyed the story!

So I didn't buy any seeds last year. The field part of the garden was a dismal failure. The dugout was too low to bother setting up a watering system way down there, the potato bugs had to be sprayed three times, the corn and the beans froze, and the peas averaged about three to a pod (but it did make for a lot less work picking and freezing). This year I will stick to my city garden idea. In fact, I ordered smaller packets of corn, peas, and beans, so I won't get carried away. The seeds came about a month ago, and I put them away immediately—in the linen closet. I know for sure that I will remember where they are, and if I don't I can just ask anybody in the district!

Garden Gloves

There is a trace of black under my nails again;
　　My fingers are rough from the earth.
I have garden gloves to wear—neat canvas gloves.

I put them on this morning
　　Before I started transplanting
Lobelias, petunias, snapdragons, moss roses,
　　Opening little hollows in the damp dark earth,
Teasing baby plants out of plastic cribs,
　　Tucking their feet in, patting their covers down,
Seeing in the tender green a rainbow promise.

I must go get my gloves.
　　I think I left them near the garden shed.
　　　　They are still neat and clean.

Eileen and Evert's wedding—best man Don Frost and bridesmaid,
sister Carolie (Kopperud) Haug, in the background, 14 January 1949.

❧

I Remember

Fifty years is a long time, but it is not as long as it used to be. In our great-grandfather's time, fifty years was the average life expectancy—for men that is. For women, it was even less. Ev and I were married fifty years ago, and a lot of things have changed since then, not to mention weddings. Things were a lot less expensive, and much more down-to-earth.

The winter of 1949 was snowy. Big drifts and blocked roads made travel difficult. Several days before 14 January, our wedding day, Uncle Arvid and several other neighbours ploughed snow off the roads leading to the church near Cadillac, and hoped they would stay passable until after the wedding. About a week before the wedding, Dad and I butchered a pig. Mom intended to serve a roast pork dinner to the whole community in the church basement, with the help of aunts who offered to make scalloped potatoes. It had to be dinner because South Immanuel had no electricity for lights, and many of the wedding guests—the invitation list included the entire community—travelled with horses, so all the business of the day had to be done before nightfall. That meant that the ceremony was at the unfashionable hour of eleven in the morning.

We were married on an unfashionable Friday, too, because on Thursday Ev and his mom, Don Frost (the best man), and Ev's Uncle Morton, Aunt Ragna, and three-year-old cousin Christine came by train, and we all had to get back to Mitchellton and Moose Jaw the same way on Saturday. Dad, cousin Earl, and I went to meet the train in Cadillac late in the afternoon on Thursday. It took two cars to transport the six people, their luggage, and the wedding flowers the seven miles home. It was less crowded than we expected because Ragna and Morton's luggage, including all their dress-up outfits, nightclothes, shaver, and toothbrushes, didn't get put off the train, but instead travelled on to Shaunavon. It wasn't much consolation to be told that the stationmaster would make sure it was put off in Cadillac on the way back the next day, just about the time the ceremony started. Mom had supper ready for us all, and then Uncle Morton and his family went to spend the night at cousin LaVerne and Earl's house. LaVerne and Ragna washed up whatever they could of the travelling clothes. Anyone who rode the train in those days will remember that it was not a good place for keeping clothes looking fresh and dainty, especially those of a toddler.

On Friday we woke up to sunny, calm, and mild weather. Dad ferried the food and most of the household to the church, and then came back to take my sister Carolie, who was my bridesmaid, and me. We didn't want to squash our dresses, of course.

I can't remember much of the ceremony. Aunt Mina sang "Crown with Thy Benediction," and the rest of the music was congregational singing, which meant that it was pretty good, as South Immanuel was noted for its great singing. There wasn't any "you may now kiss your bride" in the service so we waited for that until after the recessional. Everybody filed past us at the back of the church and gave us handshakes, kisses, good wishes, and blessings on their way downstairs to dinner. Before we went downstairs we had pictures taken inside the church and also on the back steps in the sun.

After dinner there were a few speeches, including one from my dad, who said that, as the first-born child, I was expected to be a boy. Carolie was supposed to make it one of each. Carl came along, and then Kay was expected to even things up. With Betty Anne they decided it was a lost cause. Now that Ev had joined the family, Dad had two sons and four daughters, and he expected someday he would have five of each.

After that, the community held a shower for us. We opened gift after gift, and received Lady Hamilton silverware, a pressure cooker, an end table, a whistling teakettle, fancy china cups and saucers, a roaster, lots of Pyrex ware—which was new then, including two coffee pots, a teapot, and about six pie plates—altogether too many things to remember now. Oh, I must mention that we got fourteen tablecloths—lacy, rayon, linen—and teacloths of every description. We are still using some of them. After opening the gifts, we both said our thank-yous and everybody started packing up to go home.

Later, Mom provided another good meal for about fourteen people, and at last the long day ended. Ev and I found cornflakes in our bed, so we sneaked into the kitchen through the bathroom and shook the sheet out on the kitchen floor while everyone else was still in the dining room.

The weather had deteriorated by the next morning. Dad and Earl took everyone to Cadillac to catch the eleven o'clock train. We located Uncle Morton's and Aunt Ragna's straying suitcases and loaded everything on the train. Ev's dad and a neighbour, Percy Frost, met us with a team and sleigh to make sure we had a way to get home if the car didn't start after sitting two days at Dunkirk station, seven miles north of Mitchellton. However, it did start and we took it as far as Frost's where Lucy had a lovely supper ready for us. By then there was a pretty good storm going on, so we left the car and went as far as Ev's folks' place in the sleigh.

The storm didn't let up, so we had to stay there for several days. It was not the most exotic honeymoon, I must say. We finally arrived at our new home, which was actually a very old one. (Ev and his dad had relined the old house with ten-test, put in new windows, and re-excavated the cellar.) Shortly after dark, when we had unpacked and tried to straighten things out, there was a knock at the door. Margaret and Rufus Taylor, from just across the road, had walked over to welcome us. I made coffee and cut up some wedding cake, the only baking that we had. It was not the most appropriate dainty as Margaret had just had her teeth pulled, so she couldn't chew a thing. She just laughed about it.

We started early experiencing the "make-do, make over, or do without" recycling style that has been a large part of our life, and which is now considered quite the right way of doing things. The wind and snow kept whistling in through every little cranny, so for the first several weeks in our new home Ev spent a lot of time stuffing the wrapping paper from the wedding gifts in the cracks around the windows and door.

Beautiful Hands

Slender fingers, tapered nails,
Smooth, soft, white.
A display rack for bright enamels, rings, bangles.
Graceful, idle, expensive hands.

Calloused palms, a scar or two still bright,
Short square nails that can't be scraped quite clean;
Living tools, deft and quick, reliable and strong,
Hands that are more gentle than they seem.

Old hands, brown-flecked, raised veins,
Too stiff for petit point, they still can mend,
Or flick a splinter from a baby's knee,
Smooth away pain, knead and form a loaf.

The eye of the beholder, wisdom claims,
Sees beauty unconfused.
My eye finds beauty in hands well used,
A history of service, scarred with love.

To the Ladies

It is a common assumption that during the Depression of the thirties, prairie women were a grey, defeated lot. Although it is true that there were dust storms, poor crops, and low prices for what farmers produced, that medical conditions often went untreated, debts piled up, and some families gave up, packed, and moved towards brighter prospects, that is not the whole story. The farmers who stuck it out, and later saw better days, owed a lot to their ladies. Desperation was often near, but the spirit, valour, and ingenuity of these women should not be forgotten. Defeated and grey? No way!

Boule Creek, my home district, lies south and west of Cadillac, which was the centre of the Dust Bowl. Boule Creek was also the home of the Humdinger Club, a social group that put on three-act plays, organized schoolhouse dances, and held winter house parties every two weeks. All winter long, neighbours would hitch up their teams, load up their families, and gather at one house or another to play whist, bridge, or party games. I remember a summer trip when we all piled into the back of a big truck to spend a weekend tenting at Cypress Hills. Who directed the plays, provided the games and the lunch, and kept the community alive? The ladies.

Poverty is often grubby and dirty. We may have been broke, but we didn't feel poor. "Soap is cheap and water is free," so they say, but that expression had to be modified in our area where water was pretty scarce and of poor quality.

The ladies learned to soften a barrel of hard water with a couple of tablespoons of lye the night before washday, and the laundry rinse water ended up on the peony patch, after it had been used to scrub the kitchen. When it came to soap, the ladies saved all the suet from butchering, and lard and drippings from the kitchen, bought a can of lye, and made their own. It was pretty strong stuff and was only used on the skin in absolute emergencies, but it got clothes clean and worked wonders on floors and walls.

Groceries were pretty spartan, consisting of just the essential staples, with an occasional box of apples, and sometimes a round little box of Copenhagen snoose as extras. Mr. Buckwold, the storekeeper in Cadillac, usually tucked a wee bag of hard candy into the groceries as his treat for the kids. I remember that once, on his way home from hauling grain, Dad splurged and bought a big basket of Concord grapes for us. It cost seventy-five cents, and no grapes since can compare to their memory. But we didn't go without treats. At berry-picking time, the ladies made chokecherry jelly and syrup, and occasionally even choke-cherry wine. Old-fashioned long-necked bottles were scoured and filled with root beer. At ten cents a bottle, pop was too expensive, and anyhow, we preferred the bubbly root beer. It was supposed to be good for you, too—something about roots and herbs. I remember Mom's horror and indignation when, armed with Grade Eleven biology, I informed her that root beer was alcoholic. It seemed to me if sugar and yeast were involved, alcohol would be the result, but I pulled in my horns when I realized that she might quit making it if I convinced her.

The ladies canned beef, chicken, garden vegetables, rhubarb and strawberries, rhubarb and saskatoons, rhubarb relish, and plain rhubarb fruit, as well as pickles, jam, jelly, and anything else they could get their hands on. They helped cure bacon and hams, made cheese and butter, and baked bread. On hot summer Sundays they concocted ice cream mixtures, got the men to fetch ice from the ice house, and allowed us kids to turn the freezer handle.

The budget only allowed for inexpensive store-bought material, at a dollar for three or four yards of printed cotton or flannelette, but with the help of packets of dye, some innovative ideas, and a lot of work, the ladies turned bleached flour and sugar sacks into aprons, blouses, and underwear. Occasionally the sacks turned up as frilly kitchen curtains, or embroidered kitchen tea towels and pillowcases, and sometimes they were pieced together for bed sheets or quilt backs. In spite of the legendary jokes about Robin Hood staring out from the bottom of bloomers, I never saw any that weren't bleached snowy white.

Recycling was a matter of course, long before it became fashionable. The ladies saved the buttons, then ripped the seams of clothing that didn't fit, or that was worn out in spots but still had good bits left, and made new outfits for their kids. I once had a made-over coat that had twenty-two pieces in it. They cleaned and reshaped old felt hats, brightening them up with a bit of ribbon or an artificial flower saved from something else. Rags and remnants too far gone for anything else ended up as braided or hooked rugs to add warmth and colour to old linoleum floors.

In their spare time—and I find it difficult to believe that they had any—the ladies did their bit to brighten up their homes. They pieced quilt tops, washed and carded raw wool to pad them with, put it all together on quilt frames, and invited the neighbour ladies over for an afternoon of quilting. If the top material was too heavy for little quilting stitches it would be tied, often with wool yarn reclaimed by unravelling the least worn parts of old sweaters. My grandma made beautiful quilt tops, and we slept under her cozy comforters, the same kind of comforters that nowadays are priced at one thousand dollars or more in trendy craft stores.

Education was as valued as it was hard to get. For many of us, quitting school wasn't an option. Mothers helped with high school correspondence courses and insisted that somehow we were going to finish school. If there wasn't someone in the family who could teach us to play an instrument, mothers traded butter and eggs so their children could get music lessons.

Who were these formidable women? Where did they come from? Well, most of them were home grown, or from nearby districts. A little yeast was added when young farmers married the only imports, the local schoolteachers. Three of my grandmother's four sons married teachers, a practice that made for cross-fertilization of ideas and dreams—and dreamers they all were. They made the most of what was available, and hoped for a brighter future for their loved ones. Life handed them lemons and they made lemonade. So I propose a toast. Take a glass of lemonade and let us drink—to the ladies.

The Midnight Visitor

LIVING WITH NATURE IS NOT ALL IT'S CRACKED UP TO BE

When Ev and I got married in 1949, we moved onto a half-section farm with an old ramshackle house that had not been lived in for the previous twenty-some years. The living room and a tall attic above it were over an earth cellar that Ev and his dad had re-excavated the fall before. The rest of the house, kitchen, and bedroom were in a lean-to addition. There was no foundation, only earth banking thrown up around the whole thing. It sounds grim, but with new windows and the walls freshly panelled with ten-test, it was pretty cozy. Oh, when it rained, the lean-to roof leaked, we could hear mice playing leap-frog over the rafters at night, and we did spend the first couple of weeks of our married life stuffing cracks around the windows with wedding-present wrapping paper to keep the snow from sifting in, but in those days young folk didn't expect to start out with all the amenities.

That spring we borrowed a brooder house and got a hundred day-old chicks. I could keep a good eye on them as they started to lose their baby down, because the brooder house was only about twenty yards from the house, on one of the few flat spots in the yard.

About twelve o'clock one night I woke to hear definite digging sounds. I immediately decided that a badger was digging under the brooder house, intending to feast on my wee chicks. Ev lit the lantern, loaded the shotgun, put on his rubber boots, and went to the rescue.

It was chilly in the house so I hopped back into bed. He had barely shut the door when there was a tremendous boom that shook the walls and rattled the windows. Seconds later the essence of skunk wafted through our home. Then I heard his rubber boots pounding away towards the barn at a dead gallop. I got up and peered out into the darkness. I said, out loud, "That crazy nut has shot under the house and killed a skunk. We will never get it out." I couldn't see a thing, but I could hear his rubber boots whumping back to the house and then away again. What in the world was going on?

Ev came in a few minutes later and explained. Just after he had shut the door and turned the corner, he'd stopped dead. A big skunk was looking him right in the eye. He had to set the lantern down before he could shoot, and in the interim the skunk shot first. Luckily, the skunk was also in a hurry and missed him, but hit the wall and all the earth banking on that side of the house. The whumping sound was Ev racing to the barn for a fork, running back to pick up the dead skunk, and then going away again to get it as far from the house as he could.

As we talked, our eyes began to smart and tears ran down our faces. Opening the windows was no help at all; in fact, it made the smell even worse. With the windows shut the air was breathable, barely.

Somewhere from the vast store of mostly useless information that is packed into my head, I remembered that vinegar was supposed to be good for destroying odours, so I filled saucers with all the vinegar I had and set them here and there through the house. I lit a perfume lamp. We smoked cigarettes. Nothing really helped. For several days the odour in the house still had the power to make our noses run and our eyes burn.

I guess our noses finally refused to register the skunk smell because it stopped bothering us, although visitors commented on it all summer. When we went to visit my folks for a couple of days we could smell it again when we got back. The chicks grew up and eventually ended up in sealers—the canned chicken smelled great.

Ev scraped the top layer of the banking off and replaced it with fresh soil, but for years afterwards a good rain would reactivate the essence of skunk and, until the ground dried out, remind us of our midnight visitor.

Sea Biscuit during one of his many "train-yet-*another*-rider" sessions.

Biscuit

A TALE OF A FOUR-LEGGED FRIEND
WHO BECAME PART OF THE FAMILY

What our son Lyle really wanted was a motorcycle. What he got was a horse, and a big one at that. Sea Biscuit was tall, black, and frisky. Lyle, twelve years old, was tall and pretty frisky, too—a good match, I thought. The horse's name was soon shortened to just Biscuit, and the two developed a deep attachment for each other.

When Lyle was little he was undecided about whether he wanted to be a cowboy or an Indian when he grew up. After he got Biscuit, Grandpa and Nan gave him a saddle for Christmas, so he settled for entering the 4-H Light Horse Group. There were seven or eight in that class and most of them had quarter horses, which were smaller and quicker. It really didn't matter except on Achievement Day, when the judge was usually a "quarter-horse man." I am not sure how much Biscuit got out of the 4-H classes, but Lyle learned quite a bit, including that owning a horse involved some work and was not all galloping around through the landscape.

It was pretty easy in summer, when Biscuit had the run of a small pasture with a dugout. A few minutes grooming and petting, and putting out some oat chop for a treat was about all the work involved then. In winter it was a different story. Every morning before the school bus came, Lyle had to dress warmly, feed and water his charge, and keep the stall in the old barn clean and bedded. I often felt sorry for him as I watched him make his way out into the early dark morning. He seldom fussed about it, and developed a good sense of responsibility.

One fall, Lyle rode Biscuit bareback to the frozen pond to chop out a drinking hole for him. It wasn't that far, but why walk when you can ride? (My kids even took their bikes when they made a trip to the outdoor toilet.) After the watering, Lyle went to jump back on Biscuit's back, just as the horse became startled at something and jumped around. Lyle, encumbered by the hatchet, went right over the horse and landed on his shoulder, breaking a collarbone and dislocating his shoulder. Stoically, he led Biscuit back to the barn, tied him in his stall with one good hand, then came to the house, white-faced and tight-lipped. We took him to emergency, where he was X-rayed and strapped up. For several months his dad took over the chores, which I suppose was some sort of compensation for Lyle.

One spring Lyle took his .22 rifle to the far end of the pasture to shoot at some gophers that had moved in. When I looked out a little later, Lyle was lying flat in the long grass, and so was Biscuit. With horrible visions of both of them shot, I started running out there, shouting and yelling. The wind was blowing against me, so they didn't hear me for a while. When I got closer they both raised their heads, swivelled their necks, and looked to see what the commotion was all about. They were fine. Biscuit had followed Lyle, and when Lyle lay down to wait for an inquisitive gopher to poke its head out of its burrow, Biscuit decided it must be nap time, so he lay down, too.

Lyle finally got his motorcycle, and then went away to high school at Outlook, but by that time his brother, Keith, and sister, Karen, were old enough to enjoy riding. Biscuit went through another 4-H class with Keith.

As he got older, the horse became pretty wise and crafty. He was still frisky when his rider was experienced, but when we put young visitors on his back, all their giddy-upping and heel-nudging only made him glance back curiously as he continued a slow, steady plod around the pasture. The only way he would trot was if a grown-up took his lead rope and ran ahead of him, sort of a towing job. Grown-ups quickly lost their enthusiasm for brisk trots around the pasture, so Biscuit had it pretty easy.

Eventually the children grew up and left home, and Biscuit grew older. We had chances to sell him several times, but by then he had become so much a part of the family that we would have felt we were selling one of the kids. Whenever Ev tried to fix a piece of machinery in the pasture, Biscuit supervised, nudging him once in a while to get a pat, and ignoring suggestions to move, or at least to quit snorting down Ev's neck. About the only inconvenience he endured was the yearly inoculation against mosquito-borne sleeping sickness.

One especially lush spring he overate and developed founder, a condition that makes a horse's feet become painfully inflamed. He limped pathetically and was ridden no more. He spent the rest of the summer padding around the pasture. As the weather got colder, he became stiff, sore, and even lamer. Life was no longer good to him. We were heart-sore. Like birth, death is a part of farm life that cannot be evaded, so, as hard as it was to do, Lyle put him out of his pain. Biscuit lies buried in a little hollow in the pasture behind the house, where he reigned for so many years.

Saving Stuff

There are two ways by which most of we "children of the thirties" can be identified. One is a dread of debt, especially that incurred by mortgages. The other characteristic is even more widespread: we save stuff.

Recycling is second nature to most of us. After all, didn't we invent or at least were raised under the slogan "Wear it out, use it up, make it do"? A corollary of this saying is "You never know when it may come in handy." These mottoes have become articles of faith for most of us, right up there with the Ten Commandments and driving on the right-hand side of the road.

What it leads to is clutter. I know. While waiting for good harvest weather I have been driven to cleaning out hell holes—not all of them, but a couple of obvious ones like the garden shed and the basement storage room. I had my husband's help, but he also saves stuff, so it became even more difficult to sort out and discard the useless (and so very little of it *is* useless).

I don't have a box labelled "string too short to use," but I have boxes of: (a) every button that adorned every piece of clothing that has been recycled into "useful rags" since we were married, and our parents' button collections, acquired after they died; (b) used gift wrap that isn't too wrinkled, ribbon bows that only need a bit of new Scotch tape to reattach, and cards that are too pretty to throw away—that means nearly all of them; (c) odd shapes of material left over after sewing, which may someday be useful for quilts, doll clothes, patches, or pot holders—that I have lots of quilts, no little girl grandchildren, hate patching, and can only use two pot holders at a time is irrelevant; (d) odd pieces of ribbon, lace, elastic, bias tape, interlining, and so on, a lot of which were bought at sales because they were such a great bargain, but very few of which are the colour or size I need when I do want a bit of ribbon, lace, elastic, bias tape, interlining, etc.; (e) about four pounds of zippers that have been removed from throwaways or bought at sales; and (f) yardage—or it is meterage now—of new material, bought at sales too good to pass up, or given to me by friends who have quit sewing and are strong-willed enough to give it away. And that is only the sewing room!

When my parents-in-law retired to the city, their farmhouse started to fill up. As our children left home, we gave them the "old but still usable" furniture we wanted to replace. As they prospered enough to replace these items, they gave them back to us! We put them in Gramp's house. Old television sets, insulation, a water bed, baby furniture, washing machines, an aquarium that leaks, windows, mattresses, collections of magazines, treadle sewing machines, space heaters, wallpaper sample books, outgrown toys and games too precious to discard, fossil collections, fridges, stoves, and more have all been stored, and often reclaimed by their owners, or the next in line.

I have no idea when we will use two large double-glazed picture windows, each with one pane cracked and gradually disintegrating wooden frames, but we have them. We also have several decrepit old granaries that can't be demolished because where would we put the various bits and pieces stored in one of them—and the forty-odd old tires with a few miles still in them that are stacked in the other? A third granary keeps oil barrels under cover and is used as our cat house in winter. They all come in handy.

About ten years ago, in a weak moment, my husband hauled several half-ton loads of stuff to the rubbish heap in the pasture. He wore a path from the shop to that heap in the next few years, going to look for a chunk of angle iron, a piece of tin to patch mouse holes, or a little bit of plywood so he didn't have to cut into a bigger piece.

I am improving. I can now throw out plastic meat trays, some cardboard boxes, various glass jars that don't have reusable lids, stray Barbie legs, and those ultra-thin plastic bags that apples and tomatoes come in from the grocery store. I feel a bit guilty, but I can do it.

As far as the rest of the stuff is concerned, I have a vision. When we have passed on to our reward, I am going to sit up there on a convenient cloud, and watch my children as they excavate our hidey-holes. As they sort and discard, and wonder why in the world anyone would keep this or that, I'll smile. It will make up for every small irritation and aggravation they have caused me over the years. And just think—what a garage sale they will be putting on!

Miniature

From computer chips to cars, the whole world today is enthralled with making things smaller. And I am stuck with it.

When they were little kids, Lyle and Keith had polar opposite opinions on toys. Keith was into arranging Fort Apache with eighty-seven wee Indians and cavalrymen, or making a medical kit for G.I. Joe out of a tin Aspirin box, tiny rolls of bandages, and a hypodermic syringe—a straight pin with Scotch tape rolled around the middle for the barrel. Miniatures had no place in Lyle's world; he wanted *big* trucks and earthmovers, big enough to ride on if possible. I am beginning to see Lyle's point of view.

There is a lot of talk about fine print on contracts. It is supposed to contain all kinds of little traps and snares that are sure to surprise—unpleasantly. Well, contracts only come up once in a while around here, but every few days I get frustrated by the teeny-weeny, pale words printed on everyday medicine labels—eye drops, nasal spray, tubes of salve, and even on things like mosquito repellent and sunscreen lotion. I suppose it is possible to survive without reading all this miniature stuff, but what if it's a warning? Something like, "If used more than three days in succession this substance may cause the nose to turn orange and develop warts." I believe in reading labels.

Whether they apply to fashion, home decorating, or landscaping, modern rules for style go something like "less is more." Well, not in my case. When God made me, He was generous. I notice it especially when I use public transportation—I don't fit. I will admit to an increase in width in the last several decades, but surely my legs haven't grown longer, and there are many of us long people. I still fit sideways, thank goodness, but when I get on a plane my knees snug right up into the next guy's back rest. I wiggle and squirm, and I can forget about crossing my knees. In the interest of packing a few more bodies on each flight, someone has miniaturized the seats.

We drive a full-sized van or a farmer half-ton, so miniature cars don't affect me. (They are cute, aren't they? Just about the size of Lyle's pedal car when he was three.) Mind you, graceful is not a word that comes automatically to mind when I enter or exit a little car. But my law-abiding husband—who doesn't even cut across the painted lines, and stops at deserted stop signs in an empty parking lot—has a terrible time fitting the wheels of our vehicle between the lines meant for much smaller cars. We always have to look for three empty spaces, so we can get the doors open.

A lot of advertising is big and bold (and loud, but that is another story). In television ads sports cars and half-tons end up looking immaculate after improbable journeys to improbable destinations. However, I wonder if anyone has ever deciphered the half screen of miniature print at the end of those ads. It flashes on and off in about two seconds and makes me very suspicious. So far I have read to about halfway on the second line. It contains the phrase "certain restrictions apply." I will keep trying, and in a couple of years I should know what the restrictions are. I will keep you informed.

Now big is not always better. I am glad there aren't any giant dinosaurs left, and that my computer takes up a desktop, not a suite of rooms, the way computers started out. I do think that the people who set standards should keep in mind that small can be dangerous at times. There seems to be a law of nature that the smaller things are, the more vicious they are. Miniature dogs have voices (and sometimes tempers) in inverse ratio to their size. Black flies, mosquitoes, wood ticks, and "no-see-ums" are bad enough, but look at the havoc that wee invisible germs can wreak. Viruses are even smaller and deadlier. One's chance of survival is better with a grizzly bear than with the hanta virus. There is a certain irony when we find that a mouse is more dangerous than a bear.

I take comfort in the probability that sometime soon the fashion pendulum will swing back. Long skirts come and go, hair styles go from beehive to practically bald. Car seats and parking spaces can't get any smaller, so the only way is up. Just think, then I will be fussing about how hard it is to parallel park a twenty-seven-foot car with immense fins.

Evert Comstock, sons Lyle (right) and Keith (left), and daughter-in-law
Jan during a break in the action at harvest.

❧

The Distaff Side of Harvest

WHAT EVERY FARM WOMAN KNOWS
ABOUT HELPING WITH THE HARVEST

About the middle of August, harvest fever starts on our farm. The combine is moved in front of the shop to be inspected from the pickup to the straw spreader. Chains, belts, walkers, gaskets, fans, bearings, sensors—a thousand and one things must be checked out. Then the list of parts that are needed right now, or might be needed soon, or may not be needed but take a very long time to get, is taken to the equipment agency. The bill is magnificent, in the sense of being large and awe-inspiring.

Meanwhile, the kitchen is an assembly line that is producing a month's worth of casseroles, buns, and desserts for the freezer. Every once in a while the cook is called on to be assistant mechanic. This doesn't usually take much skill, and often involves pumping brakes or standing outside the combine on tiptoe, holding a bolt at arm's length while the nut is being tightened from someplace within its bowels.

Rain, so eagerly awaited in June and July, is not wanted; about the only thing less welcome is hail. Every cloud is looked on with suspicion. We may miss *Jeopardy*, or *Home Improvement*, or the *National*, but we always catch the weather forecast.

We use a one-ton Fargo truck to haul grain from combine to bin. It is dependable, easy to back up, and reasonably comfortable. Unlike the cool comfort of the glassed-in combine cab, it has no air conditioning, but with open windows and a fan it isn't bad when you are on the move. Sitting waiting for a load gets uncomfortable, but air-conditioning doesn't work unless the motor is running, and you just *don't* leave the motor running when you are sitting in the field. Dry stubble is very easily set on fire, and then you will know what "hot" is. Open windows mean biting flies and mosquitoes, so I keep a fly swatter right next to the fire extinguisher in the truck cab.

Before we got the two-way radio, instructions from the boss (usually my husband) consisted of putting out the augur when he was ready to dump, or flicking the lights at night, as well as a variety of hand signals, none of which make sense to the trucker. I am not alone in my frustration with sign language. Donna, a young friend who was trucking for her brother-in-law, said, "One more hand wave and I will ram the back of the combine—on purpose!"

Oh, we wives are pretty good at trucking, even if we do exasperate our spouses. Those of us with larger trucks can pick up "on the go," that is, drive alongside while the grain is being unloaded from the still-moving combine. A one-ton box is too small for that and has to be manoeuvred into just the right place, depending on the slope, the wind, and the speed of the augur. We learn to estimate how many bushels we unload, test for moisture, take samples, keep track of how full the granary is, record the yield, keep the loader motor fuelled up, carry out meals, and find stuff in the shop that the boss needs—right now. It is a standing joke among the women that farmers should swap wives in harvest. They would probably be a lot more tactful with someone they weren't married to.

In spite of all the overhauling and checking beforehand, breakdowns do occur. While our husbands dismantle stuff in the field, we are sent to town for repairs. We go equipped with the model and year of the machine, the part number and position (right or left side), and are shown the part in question before we leave, if we can't carry it with us. Heaven help both us and the parts man if we bring home the wrong thing. Parts men used to be very cavalier with

women, implying that we didn't know what we wanted—
and not much else either. They are much better now, especially if, with luck, the parts man turns out to be a parts
woman.

On a warm breezy evening it is tempting, but not too
smart, to keep on harvesting long after dark. After a long
day we get mesmerized and stupid, and that is when accidents happen—and other things. I haven't been too keen
on unloading at night since one occasion when we kept on
well after sunset at our other farm, where there was no
electricity. Ev told me to use the lights of the half-ton, so I
could see to back into the loader and get everything going.
I did that and then moved away out of the dust. All of a
sudden I noticed that the grass around me was moving.
Dozens and maybe even hundreds of mice were scurrying
and skittering around me. I tucked the legs of my slacks
into my socks and sat on the half-ton fender until the truck
was empty. Then I shut the loader off and went back to the
combine to resign for the evening.

Last fall, age, arthritis, and heat caught up with me. Keith
and Jan made arrangements to come home for harvest,
with Jan taking over the trucking. I had very mixed emotions, feeling gratitude and relief, of course, but also hidden
in my heart were disappointment and resentment. Surely
no one else could really replace me, with my thirty-some
years of skill and experience. Well, harvest started a couple
of days before they could come, so I ended up out in the
truck for a while anyway—and it was too hard for me, especially for my aching knees. I gratefully relinquished the
steering wheel to my daughter-in-law, and she did just great!
No problems at all, although when Lyle also came home to
help and combined so Keith could learn to run the swather,
Jan found out what every farm woman knows. It is better to
truck for someone you aren't married to.

❧

Frustration

It has been a weird year for us farmers. Who would ever think that we would look at a cloud-filled summer sky and hope the coming rain would miss our fields? How often have farmers whose land is as flat as a baseball diamond wished they had hills and sloughs? When before did we ever want hotter days in July? In Saskatchewan?

In past years when we needed a shower there were several tried-and-true ways of bringing it on. We could clean the windows or take the van through the car wash. Before we had a clothes dryer, hanging out a big wash would usually do the trick. Even watering the garden worked occasionally. It should work in reverse, but it doesn't.

I never thought I would see the day when my farmer husband yearned to get at his summerfallowing—a boring job at best. We are about halfway through the second time over. By the time it was dry enough to start, the growth was so lush that the cultivator was useless, so Ev had to resort to the diskers. At that we are lucky because in some areas the sodden land won't support heavy machinery. Some people have bought or rented rotary mowers to try to knock the greenery down before it goes to seed. My brother-in-law swathed some of his stubble fields and hoped that the swaths would dry enough to burn. He was out with a propane torch the last time I talked to my sister Kay.

Winter feed could be a problem this year. Most summers, people are out haying the sloughs and ditches to augment what they grow as forage. Well, the sloughs are still full of water and look as if they will stay that way. The grass and alfalfa in the ditches and fields looks lush and heavy, but there hasn't been the three or four days of fine weather in a row to cut, cure, and bale it. Rain on the cut hay leaches out a lot of the nutrients, and turning the swaths to dry means that a lot of the leaves, the best part, are lost. There isn't much that can be done about it either. Baling damp hay invites mould, which affects the health of animals, and also causes it to heat up, with the resulting fire hazard.

Of course, the big farm problem is financial, and that is something that won't change no matter what the weather does. Farmers are taking on more land, diversifying, and increasing productivity, just to try to make ends meet. Fertilizer, pesticides, fuel—all the inputs that make this possible—are increasing in cost at astronomical rates. We are in a bind and have no room to manoeuvre when disasters occur.

Our problem is shared by the rest of our fellow citizens. Ask the storekeepers, automobile and machinery dealers, service industries, any businessperson—they will all say the same thing. If we go under, so will they. Frustrating, isn't it?

Evert Comstock (left), son Lyle (middle), and uncle Eldon Comstock
after a successful hunt, circa 1955.

Hunting

THE FALL HUNT IS AN ANNUAL RITUAL ON OUR FARM

Hunting season is over on our farm for this year. Two nice white-tail bucks are in the shop, hanging from the Ford tractor's bucket, and the big deal today will be getting them neatly into the back of the half-ton so we can take them to Moose Jaw to be cut up. It's really a two-man job, but Lyle had to go back to North Battleford to work yesterday.

Ev and Lyle hunted for more than four days before they got lucky. Each day they got up early, drove away before dawn, came back for a quick dinner, and didn't get home again till after dark. They drove over stubble fields and rocky pastures to places where years of experience told them deer were apt to be found. They walked through brush and long grass, uphill and down, in their heavy boots and orange coveralls. Oh, they saw deer—they even shot at a couple—but as Lyle said, "Davy Crockett and Dan'l Boone couldn't hit a thing." Every evening I heard about all their frustration before an early bedtime brought on by the cold and unaccustomed exercise. But they were having fun, they assured me. If they were forced to work that hard on a job, they would have felt greatly abused.

I think hunting is sort of like travel—more fun to talk about afterwards than when you are actually doing it. Like when they took Keith, age twelve, with them for the first time. Ev and Lyle each got off one shot. Ev's deer collapsed while Lyle's took off over the hill, with Lyle in hotfooted pursuit of his target. Ev and Keith hurried to bleed the downed deer. Ev had just straddled the deer and grabbed its antlers to pull up its head, when the deer came to. It had been grazed just above the nose and was only knocked out, not dead. It was quite a rodeo with Ev hanging on to antlers with both hands, yelling for Lyle to come back and help. Keith volunteered to go get the gun, but his dad vetoed that strenuously—he was in enough trouble already. Lyle did get back before Ev had to let go, so they got their deer.

There is a lot of breast-beating about the whole subject of hunting. Hunters are pictured as slavering monsters by people whose closest approach to nature is mowing the lawn. "How can you kill such a beautiful animal and call it 'Sport'?" they say. It *is* pretty nice to see a few deer meandering through the yard, or a mother and her twin fawns ambling around in a hay slough. There are unseeded spots in many fields where a farmer has carefully manoeuvred his equipment around a newborn fawn. We take it for granted that there will be trampled spots in our grain, usually in the best part of the field, where deer have bedded down for the night. It is another story, though, when deer foul expensive and scarce hay so cattle won't eat it, destroy piles of grain stored in temporary bins, eat gardens or every branch of newly planted fruit trees, or mutilate slow-growing spruce and pines in our shelter belts. Lawn-mowing city-dwellers may appreciate a deer's beauty, but we farmers get to appreciate the whole animal.

I have no time for slap-happy morons who get boozed up and shoot at anything that moves, or those who quit following an injured animal when the going gets tough, or waste good food by taking the head and leaving the meat in the field. Most hunters are responsible and try to get their animals as humanely as possible. It should be remembered that nature is not kind; rarely does any wild animal die a natural death. Thousands of deer and antelope starved to death last winter, surely a less easy death than being shot. Even more shocking is the fact that if a weak, old, or ill animal goes down, crows peck at its eyes and coyotes or wolves chew on it before it is dead. Even at that, a deer or antelope has a lot better chance of living out its natural life span than does a steer, hog, or chicken.

For several weeks before the hunting season opens we go "deer spotting," driving around on harvested fields and up and down country roads, recalling who lived on the now-abandoned farms. We check out the lakeshore and marvel at flocks of swans, geese, and ducks that stop here on their way south. Deer don't stay put, so I don't know how much good spotting does, but it is a sort of fall ritual. It used to be Ev and his dad, now it's Ev and me or one of our kids who spend long days together—kind of a bonding time, I guess.

After the hunters are successful comes the least appreciated part—the butchering, always a cold, messy, smelly job. One year the boys thought they would "gross out" Jan, our new daughter-in-law, by getting her to help. It didn't work. Jan is an operating-room nurse and could take a lot more "gross" than they were handing out.

It is nice to vary our menu through the rest of the year with venison chops, steaks, hamburger, and delicious sausage. If we end up with more than our family can use, the food bank gets a donation, and the hides are donated to the Saskatchewan Wildlife Association to be used in Native crafts. We waste nothing, and feel no guilt in taking a tithe from nature's bounty during hunting season, in return for providing food and shelter for wild animals the rest of the year.

Planes

A TURBULENT TALE WITH A CREEPY-CRAWLY ENDING

Reports and pictures of plane disasters in full living colour on the news haven't done much to encourage people who figure if God meant them to fly, he'd have equipped them with wings—people like my husband. Ev isn't exactly afraid to fly, but he is much more comfortable knowing that if the motor quits he can step out on the ground and open the hood.

I am not all that keen on little planes, myself. My very first trip was as a passenger in a Saskatchewan Air Ambulance plane that was taking Ev to University Hospital in Saskatoon. I was far too worried about him to worry about how we were getting there. Later, when my Estevan brother-in-law took me up for a spin, I concentrated on keeping my hands relaxed in my lap and not making a fool of myself. When number two son, Keith, got his pilot's licence and took me up, I did a marvellous job of keeping cool—all the time remembering how a few years before I had talked him through learning to drive in the city. Things like "Shoulder check now," and "Just putter along, you don't have to go any faster," or "Did you see the traffic light change?" kept coming into my mind, but they didn't seem especially appropriate, so I mostly shut up.

I enjoy big planes and will get on one any chance I get, although there have been memorable moments. Our most eventful flight was from Gatwick Airport in London when my sister Carolie and I, and our daughters, Dorianne and Karen, were coming home from a holiday. In three weeks we had been in five countries, walked miles (mostly uphill), travelled on ferries, trains, and a rented bus, and were just about played out. Somehow, Dorianne set off the beepers when she went through the security check. Her face got redder and redder as she stood in full view being frisked down with wands wielded by two uniformed guards. She looked guilty as sin. The end of the search proved her innocence, but didn't ease her embarrassment. I am sorry to say that her mother and I thought the whole procedure very funny; however, we were kind enough that we tried to hide our amusement when Dorianne rejoined us.

Karen and I sat in the smokers section in the plane, while Carolie and Dorianne were farther back. We were just nicely relaxing when little lights started flashing and the voice of doom on the intercom instructed us to fasten our seat belts again and straighten up the seat backs because there was turbulence ahead. The plane shook and shuddered for quite a while. When things eased up and we had relaxed again, Carolie came forward to ask if we were okay. She was a bit miffed, I think, that we hadn't been more scared. She and Dorianne were petrified and had been praying hard through the whole thing. She said that they had probably kept the whole works of us out of the Atlantic, all by themselves. Maybe she was right.

At about that time there was a commotion ahead and to the left of us—a Winnipeg woman was having a heart attack. They really do say "Is there a doctor in the house?" but of course it was "on board" this time. Four male passengers came to volunteer their services. They laid the patient on the floor in a passage behind the cockpit and treated her with the plane's supply of oxygen, taking turns staying with her, two at a time. Unfortunately, this passageway also led to the bathrooms, so the doors to two of the four bathrooms were blocked off. Lineups formed, each liner-upper trying not to look like a curiosity seeker. They didn't want to stare at each other, either. It's hard to look nonchalant for twenty minutes when there is nowhere to direct your eyes besides the ceiling.

At lunchtime the congestion at the front made service a bit slower than usual. I got mine—a beautiful open-face beef sandwich topped with salad dressing, cress, and alfalfa sprouts—and had pretty well finished it before Karen and the rest of our row were served. Karen had just taken a bite of her sandwich when the lady next to her gasped. Out of the cress and alfalfa sprouts on her plate crawled a fat, juicy green worm. Karen stopped chewing. The lady called a steward, who was shocked and called her supervisor. The supervisor was also shocked and took the plates to the galley—the lady's, Karen's, and those from the rest of our row as well as a couple from the next row. The head steward came to our row declaring that the London catering service would be in big trouble, and offering us an alternate menu. Our appetites had suddenly disappeared, so nobody took him up on it.

After all this excitement, the rest of the flight was almost boring. In Winnipeg the doctors went back to their seats, and we sat to wait while the lady who had suffered the heart attack was taken off to an ambulance. Then we stood around the carousel to claim our luggage and then went through customs. Tired and jet-lagged, I stood in line with the rest, desperately trying not to pay any attention to a crawly sensation—somewhere in my midsection.

A stave church.

❧

The Stave Church

A few years ago my sister, Carolie, our friend, Helen, who is sort of a shirt-tail relative, and I flew overseas and joined a bus tour of Scandinavia. When our Norwegian grandparents settled on the Saskatchewan prairies they came into a country that had no past that involved them, and no memories to inherit, only vague dreams of the future to sustain them through the loneliness, hardship, and toil in their efforts to survive. They called Norway "the Old Country." As we travelled through the forests or beside the waterfalls, past the brightly painted farm buildings or through the old city streets, we three felt as if we were on a pilgrimage. It was as if we were going back to something we could almost remember.

One day as afternoon shadows were stretching long, the bus stopped at Borgund, site of the oldest wooden building in Europe. We got out to see the nine-hundred-year-old Stave Church. About a thousand years ago, the Norwegian king, Olaf Haraldson, adopted Christianity and proceeded to convert his kingdom, using rather rugged methods. With his soldiers as backup, he declared that everybody was to be baptized. The alternative was to run away into the mountains as outlaws, or be killed—almost everyone converted. For this, Olaf was made a saint. (Saints were rougher then than they seem to be nowadays.) Later, as missionaries from Europe, especially Denmark, brought the teachings of the Gospel, Christianity became accepted. The old warlike gods—Thor, Odin, Freya, and the rest—

retired to the mountains, Jotunheim, where they lived on as legends.

There were three buildings in the little forest clearing. The biggest, a church built in the 1600s when the congregation grew too large for the small church, was dismissed by our guide as of no interest—it was too new. Downhill a bit stood the old stave church and the bell tower. The bell tower was built separately because the big bell's vibrations would have shaken the pegs right out of the old wooden church. The church was a soft grey, but it was nearly time for it to be painted with black tar again, which was done every twenty years. There were over thirty steep roof surfaces that looked scaly because each shingle was rounded at the bottom. Every roof cornice sported a dragon's head hissing and spitting. I like to think that the builders of the old Viking dragon boats donated their carving skills to their new God.

Staves are the upright slabs of timber that make up the walls and give the church its name. (We use a related word when we talk of staves in a barrel.) The original church built on this spot lasted only a few years because the staves were put right on the earth. The heavy beams soon rotted from the moisture, so it was rebuilt putting stones under the timbers. The small, central room is stone-floored, too, and surrounded by a corridor where weapons were left while services were on. Lepers were allowed in the church only as far as the outer corridor. On the heavy plank door panels there was an elaborate carving of a man struggling with serpents. I wondered if the carvers had been inspired by Genesis, or Revelations, or maybe even an old pagan legend.

It was nearly dark in the old church, partly because of the time of day, and partly because there were only a few high little windows, which had been covered originally with parchment. There were no windows in the north wall. Our guide told us that evil spirits haunt the north wall of a building, so that is where the women worshippers got to stand.

The guide's torch lit up the big stone altar. This block is thought to have been recycled from its original use as a pagan sacrificial altar because it had a channel carved into it for blood to run down. Near the altar was a sliding panel that connected to the outer corridor. Through this opening the priest gave communion from a common cup to the lepers. The pyx and paten and other furnishings of the altar were stored in a jaunty little cupboard that was decorated with red and blue vertical slats, to match the pulpit. There was some graffiti on the north wall, scratches on the plaster, but because it was mostly runes—the old Norse alphabet signs—and hundreds of years old, it has become one of the added attractions.

Just before we left the hallowed old building, the guide shone his torchlight high on the thick old beams that support the central roof structure. There, carved into the very tops, were the faces of Thor and Odin where they could look down on the congregation. The forcibly converted old builders had hedged their bets.

We got back on the bus, still smiling about the trick the carvers had played. I felt so close to those people of long ago. I wonder if in our tear-down, throwaway part of the world we will ever be able to save significant things from our lives so that our descendants, a thousand years from now, will feel close to us.

❧

Stonehenge

We were heading for Stonehenge. Because, like every town in England, Salisbury had dozens of signs telling us how to get to the city centre, and not one telling us how to get out, we drove out of the town onto the wrong highway and had to do some quick map reading and angle back to the north-west with the bus. No ordinary rental car in England will hold six Canadian women and their luggage, so we had rented a small Volkswagen bus for our do-it-yourself tour. We sisters—Carolie, Kay, and I—with Dorianne, Heidi, and Karen, our daughters, had spent the previous day and a half navigating narrow highways surrounded by trees or towns. We welcomed the open Wiltshire Plains; except for the red earth, it was almost like driving in Saskatchewan.

We kept looking for the four-thousand-year-old centre of worship that, in our mind's eye, should loom on the horizon as big as the Parliament Buildings. We were kind of disappointed when it came into view—the wide expanse of prairie around it made it look a lot smaller than it does in pictures.

We pulled into the parking lot on the north side of the highway and made our way down a ramp to an access tunnel. There, under the road, are the offices, souvenir shops, and public toilets. It was there we first encountered official British toilet paper. Someplace there is somebody who manufactures the waxiest, stiffest, sturdiest toilet paper in the world, and the British Government has bought thousands of tons of it. We found it all over England, Scotland, and Wales. It would be great for wrapping lunches, writing novels, or sealing jelly jars. We took home some samples because we knew a mere description would not do it justice.

Stonehenge looked a lot bigger when we got right up to it. Because of vandalism, the central circle of stones was roped off. We could walk around the main group of stones, but not among them. They were sombre grey at first sight, but a cool, brisk wind chased the clouds around and sunbeams turned the stones a golden tan. The thirty largest stones came from twenty miles away on the Wiltshire Plains, weigh about twenty-eight tons each, and stand more than three times the height of a man; even then a third of each stone is buried in the earth. The rocks that make up the top railing have knobs that fit into notches in the uprights. There are lots of theories, but no one really knows how a people with no machinery or metal gathered, moved, shaped, and erected the massive stones. It would be a challenge today with all our modern equipment, so it's no wonder that people a thousand years ago called Stonehenge "The Giant's Dance," and thought that Merlin had transported it from Ireland by magic.

Northeast of the main circle are the remains of an avenue that once led to the Avon River. The smaller blue stones that are in the centre of the monument originated in the Prescelly Mountains in Wales, three hundred miles away. After being hauled across country they were taken by raft around the southwest corner of Wales to the Bristol Channel, then up the Severn River to the mouth of the Avon. The four-ton stones were manoeuvred around all its curves and then dragged two miles up this path. The Hele stone that marks the near end of the avenue really does have a heel mark on it. Legend has it that the devil kicked it—probably because making the monument kept people too busy to sin.

Just inside the ditch and low bank that encircle the monument are fifty-six little concrete pads marking the

Aubrey holes. These holes were dug shortly after work on the monument was started, and then they were filled in again. Again, no one really knows why, and again there are lots of theories. Charred bones were found at the bottom of a few holes when they were excavated by John Aubrey, an amateur archaeologist, so some people think they were made to hold sacrifices. One modern mathematician-astronomer thinks that they were used as a computer, and that ancient forecasters could shift rocks from one hole to another to keep track of coming eclipses.

We took pictures, read the plaques, and meandered here and there, trying to engrave the images on our minds because goodness knows if we would ever get back for a second look. The clouds thickened, the wind got brisker, and drops of rain started to dampen our enthusiasm. I mother-henned everybody together and we went back to the parking lot. Stonehenge lay behind us, grey and eerie in the rain, and looking as if it will be there for a few centuries yet.

It is almost a perfect memory. What sticks in my mind though, is the walk up the ramp on our way in. Carolie, Kay (in a blue jacket), and I had been walking side by side. I kept looking back over my shoulder trying to spot the three girls who had lingered in the tunnel. As the oldest— and the one responsible for planning the whole trip—my mother-hen reflex was working overtime. At last I saw them and said to the person in a blue jacket walking beside me, "At least, since I have come to England, I have learned to count to six." No answer. Then I realized that Carolie and Kay had lagged several yards behind me. A strange man in a blue jacket, who now was walking beside me, glanced at me warily. I could tell by the stunned look on his face that he was astonished at my cleverness.

The four Kopperud sisters (left to right: Betty, Kay, Carolie, and Eileen) ready for church.

Sisters

Sister bawls and tattles when I hardly even touched her.
  When I cup my fingers and point at her beneath them
    Sister gets upset—I didn't say a thing.
Sisters have an imaginary equator in the back seat
  That neither will let the other cross.
Sister runs for help when I can't get off the granary roof.
  Sister says "Let's tend that I'm the mommy
    And you be the little kid."
Sisters snuggle like spoons under the comforter.

Husbands discuss cars and combines after dinner
  While we sisters wash dishes and discuss our mother.
A commotion among cousins is handled by whoever's near,
  Distributing scolds or kisses and leaving peace between.
If my sister pipes, then will I dance.
  And if I mourn, she laments.
When despair pursues doubt, sister comes to be there;
  Not to fix anything, just to be there.

Now, we grandmas talk,
  Talk of children,
Grandchildren,
  Their wins and woes, their triumphs and their tumbles,
Skirting each other's sore spots,
  Remembering separate versions of family legends.
Each of us stronger. We rest secure
  On a sister's wisdom, love, compassion.

Eileen and grandson David Comstock on one of the high banks at Old Wives Lake—Eileen is probably pointing out a possible site of the "massacre."

❧

Old Wives Lake

A LESSON ABOUT MESSING WITH NATURE

There is an historic marker high on one of the Dirt Hills on Highway 2, south of Moose Jaw. The plaque tells how, several centuries ago, Cree buffalo hunters and their families, who were camped on the shore of the lake seen on the western horizon, escaped a Blackfoot raiding party. The old women urged their families to leave in darkness, while the grandmothers kept the campfires bright through the night. The Blackfeet, angry at the Crees' deception, killed the women the next morning, and threw their bodies into the lake. It is said that the old wives can be heard laughing, even yet. And that is how Old Wives Lake got its name.

There are teepee rings in nearby pastures, relics of the ancient hunters who came here for the buffalo, deer, antelope, ducks, and geese. Because of the number of hilltop grave sites, archaeologists think that the lake was a sacred place. The nomadic tribes carried the bones of their loved ones back to bury them on the surrounding hills.

On the map Old Wives Lake looks pretty impressive. About thirty miles across, it is the largest natural body of water in southern Saskatchewan. It is one of a string of saline lakes—Chaplin, Old Wives, Lake of the Rivers, and Willowbunch—that lie in a vast wrinkle on the rolling prairie, with no outlet to the sea. A network of creeks, including Pinto, Wise, Notukeu, Bull, Wiwa, Chaplin, and others, join the Wood River just before it enters the lake.

For thousands of years, these tributaries have carried mineral salts to the lake, and the hot summer sun evaporated the water and concentrated the brine. Fish can live in the creeks, in the river, and in the dams that men have built on them, but brine shrimp are about the only creatures that thrive in the lake. There are no cottages, no water skiers, and no tall trees for shade. Animals can safely drink from the lake after the spring influx, and they become inured to it through the year, although it is somewhat laxative. Cormorants and pelicans nest on the island, safe from predatory coyotes and foxes.

In periods of drought, the lake shrinks; it has receded and recovered time and again through the centuries. Man just about did it in, though. Ducks Unlimited, an American sports group, started the problem by building dams to provide breeding spots for ducks, so they could shoot more of them. Soon every little creek was dammed here and there, some for irrigating forage, some to provide drinking water for cattle, and some to create farm and village reservoirs. Then a large dam on the Wood River, south of Gravelbourg, created Thompson Lake, great for fishing, boating, golf, and cottages, as well as a water supply for adjacent residents. Soon water was being diverted from what little was left of the inflow to the lake to allow Saskatchewan Minerals at Chaplin harvesting ponds for sodium sulphate. Open winters with little snowfall only made things worse, until blinding white expanses of sodium and magnesium salt flats covered three quarters of the lake bed. The lake was useless, anyway, so who cared?

We soon found out. All of us within the wind's reach— we cared. Every breeze brought the salt with it. It piled in foot-high drifts on pastures near the lake, covering the vegetation. Trees and bushes, so hard to grow here anyway, died. As we walked through the dry grass, our shoes became white with salt. Kittens and other small animals developed sore eyes and breathing difficulties. Cattle could not be pastured; they developed pneumonia from breathing salt, and scours from eating the grass, which is not hard to understand, as magnesium sulphate is just another name for Epsom salts. Our windows were coated with salt scum; even dishes in the china cabinet were grey with it. It permeated power poles, causing short-circuits with every shower, and power failures as often as twelve times on a damp day. When the northwest wind blew, we couldn't see half a mile. We longed for water to fill that useless lake.

Slowly, salt-tolerant reeds took over some of the dry lake bed, and the next years were not as bad. Then more winter snow, increasing rainfall, and the removal of several dams helped bring some water back to the lake. The past two winters' snow and runoff have filled it once more.

We must keep trust with the lake—it may be sacred, after all. Last night I heard the loons on Old Wives Lake again. When their haunting laugh echoes back from the cutbanks on the northeast shore, it is not hard to believe that the Cree grandmothers are still cackling over the trick they played so many years ago.

Feeding time at the "zoo."

Curly Too

A VISIT FROM A SKUNK BRINGS SAD CONSEQUENCES

I am not much for having pets in the house. Oh, born and raised on a farm, I like animals. I like to see them well cared for, and I even enjoy feeding them and keeping them clean and comfortable. As for pets, I will pat their heads, but I never got involved enough to roughhouse with them, hold them in my arms, or enjoy a slobbery tongue near my face the way my kids did.

When Karen was fourteen, so was King, or Old Pup as he usually was called. Old Pup was feeling his age, nearly one hundred in dog years, and we knew he wouldn't be around much longer. Early in spring, neighbours gave Karen a cute, curly black pup. We thought Curly would make Old Pup's eventual death more bearable for Karen, who did rough-house, hold, cuddle, and allow herself to be kissed by our cats and dog. She even liked garter snakes, earthworms, and hairless baby mice, and carried them in her hand and stroked them tenderly. Ugh.

Curly was bouncy, unpredictable, and adventurous, and within a week ran directly under a visiting neighbour's car tire. So we got Curly Too, his brother, not quite as curly or bouncy but just as lovable. Curly Too, Old Pup, and three cats shared a bed in our little open porch. Old blankets and sweaters made a mattress in a big sturdy carton, cut down in front. Late one evening we heard a terrible commotion in the porch. Opening the inside door and looking through the screen, we saw three cats, two dogs, and a skunk, all in a flurry, and the skunk seemed to be winning. No odour at all, though. Ev loaded his .22. The skunk was ambling down towards the shop lights when he got it with his first shot. Ev even had the presence of mind not to hit its head, in case it was rabid.

When Ev opened the screen door to go out to shoot the skunk, Curly Too had scooted inside between his legs and made about thirteen circles around me as I stood in my long nightgown in the middle of the kitchen. As he whimpered, yelped, and circled, his bladder control evaporated, and by the time I managed to catch him I was surrounded by a very wet floor. I had no idea little dogs had such large reservoirs.

Ev put the dead skunk into a black garbage bag. We put Curly Too into a high box in the kitchen, with an old soft jacket to sleep on. I changed my nightgown. We decided that ten thirty at night was too late to call the vet, so Ev, Karen, and I finally got to bed.

The next morning, after Karen got on the school bus, Ev and I took the dead skunk to the veterinarian's office in Assiniboia, and they sent the head to be tested for rabies. It would take about three days for the results to come back. They told us if it was rabid, our pets either had to be killed, or we would have to make a cage and keep them isolated for six months with no human contact, in case they had been infected. There were no shots or medicine for animals that had become infected, although there was treatment for humans.

I spent much of the next three days holding Curly Too on my lap, stroking his soft black wavy hair and humming lullabies. The dreaded phone call came Friday morning just after Karen left for school. It was rabies.

We decided that keeping a little pup in isolation for months was impractical as well as cruel. The possibility that our child or others might be put at risk was too great to be chanced. Ev dug a deep hole in the pasture with the tractor and the front-end loader, then took the gun and did what he had to do. He laid the five animals side by side, covered them with the sweaters and blankets that had been their bed, and put all the food bowls in beside them. Then he filled in the grave.

As soon as Karen got home we took her to the animal shelter in Moose Jaw and let her pick out a pup. She didn't look at the little black ones, but chose a brown and tan Shepherd and Newfoundland cross. She called him Baney. He grew very large indeed, with feet the size of saucers, a muscular tail that could wipe out three feet of garden seedlings with one swish as he sat watching me pull weeds, and a tongue long enough to wrap around his neck.

After Karen grew up and left home, Baney stayed on the farm to take care of us. He, too, finally got old and stiff. He eventually developed cancer and was in so much pain that we had to have him put to sleep. We haven't had a dog since he went. We do still have anywhere from ten to seventeen barn cats. Ev fixes up a heat lamp and insulated tarps for their winter quarters and has built them a self-feeder that costs about four hundred dollars a year to keep stocked with three-flavour cat nibbles. We justify the expense by the fact that they keep the farm rodent-free, mostly.

I sometimes speculate that after the next ice age, archaeologists digging around in Saskatchewan to learn what manner of people lived way back when, will find what is left of Old Pup, Curly Too, and the cats, and write a scholarly treatise on how we ancients worshipped animals, the evidence being the way we buried them in woollen robes with bowls of food offerings. Maybe they won't be so far off, at that.

Petty Things

DO LIFE'S LITTLE IRRITATIONS INCREASE AS WE AGE?

Cranky, testy, out of sorts, bugged, put out, irate, unreasonable, fuming—my, aren't there a lot of ways to express the frame of mind we get into when we are irritated? Irritated—there's another one. I am usually a pleasant person. I like being pleasant, and it distresses me that as I age, I seem to find it becoming easier to be cranky, testy, out of sorts, put out, and irritable with the little things that pleasant people should be able to ignore.

It is petty things that bother me now, and I am not alone. Things like potato chip bags I can't get open, plastic toothpaste tubes that won't roll up, toilet paper rolls put on the wrong way around, bottles in the medicine cabinet with teeny-weeny writing that I can't read even with my glasses on, magazines that print the first page of articles on coloured paper, or on paper so glossy that the only thing visible is the reflection of the reading lamp. Nothing earth-shaking, only irritating.

I am a radio fan, but can anybody tell me why the only radio news item that is not repeated every hour on the hour is the one that I caught only the end of—the one that sounded so urgent and important to my well-being. And why do radio people use "less" when they mean "fewer"? I find myself scolding, "Fewer if what you are talking about can be counted, less if it is an amorphous mass—*fewer* showers, *less* rain!"

A lot of us are members of the generation that feels guilty to keep anyone waiting, so we get to appointments on time and find ourselves sitting in waiting rooms for hours with no explanation. Little announcements, like "The doctor has been called to the delivery room," or "We are trying to coax Mr. Smith in from the window ledge of the fourteenth floor. He feels that the Internal Revenue Service is out to get him," or "Miss Johnson ate poison mushrooms for dinner and is having her stomach pumped" would probably satisfy us. Speaking of waiting on doctors, why is the temperature of the examining room where you have to sit and wait, naked except for a child-sized cotton sheet, always closer to the temperature of James Bay than to that of bath water?

The telephone used to be quick and convenient. Now we phone long distance, are put on hold, and watch the expensive minutes elapse while we listen to music interspersed with a recorded voice telling us how important our call is to them. We phone for information and get a menu. All we really want is to talk to a human, and that isn't on the menu. Telephone solicitors take notice: when I want to donate, or buy something, or get my rugs cleaned, I will initiate the process, thank you. And it won't be at mealtime, or when I am having my after-dinner snooze.

I am not much of a recreational shopper. I consider it work. Even enthusiastic shoppers get aggravated when brand-new clothing has seams that aren't completely sewn, scratchy neck labels, or hems that disintegrate into a frayed edge and a long piece of fishing filament. Not that we can't fix things, but it's a nuisance. Have you ever noticed that just when you get your favourite grocery store mapped out in your mind, so that it is possible to go directly to the shelf that holds the ketchup when that's the only thing you need and you are in a hurry, somebody will have spent the preceding night entirely rearranging the whole works? We know Canada is a bilingual country, therefore there will be both French and English on labels, but why is the French side so often turned to the front in Saskatchewan? I suspect it is the cans themselves that shuffle around when nobody is looking. And I will give pretty good odds that most cans in Quebec City grocery stores face out speaking English. This is an example of the perversity of inanimate objects.

As a member of the farming community, I can safely say that the metric system is always a source of irritation, petty and otherwise. We all have to have two sets of tools because bolts and nuts, or anything else on our machinery that has to be taken off or tightened up, come in both metric and imperial sizes, and if we only take out one type of tool, we are bound to have the wrong one. Instructions for chemicals, pesticides, herbicides, and fertilizers are defined in litres per hectare. We think in acres, ounces, and quarts, and there isn't a measured hectare of land in any farmer's field in all of Saskatchewan. Oh, we have learned to convert and I suppose the required mental agility is good for our brains, but it is a nuisance. On the petty side, wind chill expressed as how fast a square chunk of metal cools off is in no way as graphic as being able to say "Put on your long drawers; with this wind chill it is minus sixty outside."

Have you ever noticed how often things that shouldn't open, do, and things that should, don't? Shoelaces come undone, zipper latches creep down, jam jar lids need a wrench, and blister packs won't open without the use of a whole tool kit. When a "some assembly needed" microwave cart or set of shelves comes with all the little screws, plugs, and latches, why are they always one screw short, and why is that one the only kind not represented in the twenty-some cans full of screws in the shop?

Then there are the people who come up to us at parties and say "I'll bet you don't remember me." They're right. And those sticky price labels that leave a gummy spot that you can't get off without demolishing the surface.

All in all, it is a tribute to the general niceness of mankind, and womankind, too, that with all the things that are put on earth to try our patience, there are so many pleasant people around.

Somebody

Somebody lives in our house and I wish they'd move away.
  They really are a nuisance and it gets worse every day.

Somebody loses bills and shoes. Somebody hid the pliers.
  Somebody left the door ajar and let in pesky fliers.

Somebody broke the china cat. Somebody lost the hoe.
  Somebody moved the furniture—last night I stubbed my toe.

Somebody runs the phone bill up, forgets to turn out lights.
  Someone spilled grape juice in the fridge and stuck the jug
    on tight.

Somebody scratched the tabletop, dropped ashes on the floor.
  Someone forgot to close the tap and let the water pour.

Somebody used the last ice cube and didn't fill the tray.
  Somebody made a shopping list, then left it where it lay.

Somebody didn't get around to cleaning up the garden.
  Someone painted windowsills and left the brush to harden.

Someone used the paper up—left new rolls on the shelf.
The TV in the empty room is playing to itself.

Someone nuked his coffee—it still sits there in the cup.
Somebody read the papers and forgot to fold them up.

Somebody's got to smarten up or out the door they'll be.
I'll heed the message well because
Sometimes—
Somebody's—
Me.

Evert Comstock and neighbours co-operate to move the entire house.

Moving

WHY WE PLAN ON RETIRING RIGHT HERE ON THE FARM

Remember the definition of mixed emotions—watching your mother-in-law driving off a cliff in your new car? I view moving house and home in about the same spirit. The anticipation of a nicer home, better job, new friends, and all the good things about a new location is seasoned by dread of the work involved.

Several years after we were married, we moved from our unelectrified farm house to a larger home in Bishopric, where I was teaching. It had both power and water, and was close enough that we moved everything over in bits and pieces. (We hadn't accumulated too much in a couple of years, anyhow.) We moved back and forth from Bishopric to the farm a couple of times, and although we did get electricity on the farm, the old house seemed to get smaller and shabbier each time we went back. So we bought another farm, complete with a larger house. Lyle, seven years old, was not enthusiastic. I was telling him about his new bedroom and a basement to play in, when he looked around wistfully and said, "But, Mom, I have spent my whole childhood here!"

I suppose every mover has the same idea as I had when I started packing. I told myself I would be very methodical. I collected cardboard cartons from the grocery store, cleaned each thing before padding it in newspaper, and made a list of contents for each box. I ran out of boxes, so I got more. I ran out of newspaper, so I scrounged more, and also started using sheets, towels, summer clothing, old drapes—anything I could find for padding. My lists deteriorated into crayoned hieroglyphics on box lids: B. Room, Bowls and pics, Kit. p&p's. I soothed my conscience by assuring myself that I had a good memory. I think at some point I must have packed my memory into one of the boxes, too, because when I desperately needed an already-packed item, I had to rummage through about six boxes to locate it.

We had to wait until near the end of November to move, and I was on tenterhooks worrying that the roads would be blocked with winter snow. I remember the moving date well—27 November 1957. A couple of neighbours brought trucks and helped with the heaving and toting. I spent the day unpacking boxes and trying to bring order out of chaos in our new house. Finally the last load came, the last box got tucked away with others I hadn't got to yet, and I revealed what I had been concealing all day. We scooted to the hospital and our second son, Keith, arrived the next morning—28 November.

By the time the kids grew up and started their turns at moving, I had almost forgotten how much commotion it involves. Of course, our truck was usually required, so we were, too. It was nice to be needed, though.

One of the more complicated events involved picking up a rental moving van in Regina in midwinter, going to Carlyle, and helping to load the van. Then Keith, Jan, Ev, and I ferried their two cars, our station wagon, and the van to Prince Albert, where everything had to be negotiated up three flights of stairs. My back kinked out early in the morning so I wasn't much help except as a driver. The only other casualty was a beautiful big dieffenbachia plant that rode in the catbird seat beside my son in the front of the moving van all day. It froze solid when the van doors were left open for unloading.

Our three kids are now firmly settled into houses that are big enough and nice enough, and they all seem to like where they are. Actually, we haven't had to help with the last few moves, which didn't hurt my feelings too much.

We still get called on to haul odd things that one or other of the family doesn't want to keep, or throw away either. Those end up stored in Gramp's old house, along with the wringer washer, the coal stove, and the stuff that Ev and I can't bring ourselves to throw away. It is surprising how much of it gets recycled.

Ev and I are getting to retirement age. Do we plan to move off the farm? Live in town? Not unless something drastic occurs to our health, we don't. I think our decision to stay on the farm is not only because we like it right here—it's because moving is just too much work.

Eileen and Evert travelling home on the train
after their wedding, January 1949.

❧

𝒯rains

On days when the air is heavy and calm, we hear the wail of the train at the Dunkirk crossing. Occasionally, when the air is so thick that you can nearly wade through it, it is possible to hear, or maybe we just feel, the chug-chug vibration of the engine, too. And that is about as close and personal as I ever get to trains, these days.

It was not always so. When I was a kid, our cans of cream, crates of eggs, cattle, and grain all went to market by train. When the radio battery was dead, Mom set the kitchen clock by the eleven o'clock train steaming across the prairie, four miles away. The local mixed train, consisting of the engine and coal car, a couple of freight cars, the mail car, one or two passenger cars, and the caboose, was our link to the outside world. Our mail—letters from Grandma Lindeblom way down in the States, the *Free Press Prairie Farm* paper, Eaton's parcels, Christmas presents from far-away aunts—all came by train. In early fall, Dad went to the train station to hire harvesters all the way from Ontario. These lads had come by train and stopped off in little prairie towns, hoping they would find work. The chairman of the school board went to the station to pick up the new schoolteacher for our little country school. The town dray met the train to pick up and deliver bulk groceries for town stores, the mail for the post office, and repair parts for the machinery dealers. Our high school Literary Society went by train to Shaunavon to perform our annual school play in their auditorium. As a young teacher, I travelled to and from my job on the train. That was how people travelled then.

It was not the most comfortable trip. In summer, the passenger cars were hot and stuffy, and if we sat beside an open window to catch a little fresh air, we also caught our fill of little smuts—soot particles from the coal-fired steam engine. In late December, the cars were crowded, as I and everyone else came home from school or work, and young soldiers came home on Christmas leave. The trains always ran late then, because of extra freight and mail that had to be unloaded at every stop.

The conductor was an "old" man; he must have been almost fifty! He punched our tickets, and at Assiniboia, when everyone trooped across Railway Street to the restaurants on each corner for lunch, he made sure we knew that we had to be back in an hour. He kept a fatherly eye on us youngsters. He made little jokes about the girlish names of the towns we were going through: May'ronne, Hazel'mor, and Ann'eroid. It was not a bad way to spend the day; we could munch on candy bars from our pockets, chat to fellow passengers, read or even nap, and the bathroom was just down the corridor.

The local mixed train is just a memory now, and even most of the tracks have been torn up. No doubt we now travel faster by car, and more dangerously too. A train didn't go into the ditch if it was icy, nor smash into other trains. I am glad that I was born early enough to remember how scarily grown-up it felt the first time I boarded the train, put my suitcase up in the luggage rack, and watched my home town disappear down the track.

Words and Weather

WHY RURAL AND URBAN FOLK
DON'T ALWAYS SEE EYE TO EYE

Because our entire income depends on what kind of weather we get from April to October, we country folk tend to be a bit touchy about comments on the radio like "A beautiful five-day forecast for the prairies; not a cloud in the sky; hot and sunny days ahead for the rest of the week and through the weekend," when our idea of a beautiful weekend is about two and a half inches in the rain gauge.

A generation ago most people in prairie cities were not so far removed from their farm roots that vocabulary was a problem. Times have changed, however. As an unrepentant stubble-jumper who admits to not having "street-smarts," and who can't imagine having neighbours that I hardly know, I get just about enough city half a day at a time. And lately I notice that we are growing apart. Maybe not as far apart as city and country were a hundred years ago, but we sometimes seem to speak a different language.

Words do not always mean the same thing once you get past paved streets. For us, a "dugout" is a hole with water in it, not a place for a ball team to sit; an "approach" is a built-up part of a ditch for machinery to get from the road to the field, not a method of getting to know a pretty girl at a party; "summerfallow" is an unpleasantly active verb, not always a noun; and "trash" is good, so long as it is on "summerfallow" (noun). "Workday" is not nine to five, but from dawn till you can't take it anymore, and in spurts when the weather is right, and "day off" means just puttering around when it isn't. A "junk pile" is not something that is waiting to be hauled away by the garbage man, but a farmer's treasure, a source of repairs, and a repository of memories, never to be spoken of in less than reverent tones. "Rape" is an oilseed to be planted and harvested, not—well, you get the idea.

Another thing I have noticed is that farmers do a lot of talking in numbers. The seven south of the house, the east eighty, the forty south of the slough are each particular fields while the back thirty may be a pasture. It behoves a farm wife to learn all those terms well, or she may find herself wandering around looking for an increasingly hungry, impatient husband. Up in the four-figure numbers are things like 2370, or 5000, both of which are tractors, while a 1460 is a combine. I am not up on all the machinery numbers, because my mind tends to wander when the talk gets that technical. Now that things are metric, I miss the horsepower numbers. The difference between a forty-horse motor and a fifty-two horse one seems a lot more concrete than the difference between a 305 and a 454. (Although I can almost figure out what half a horse would be, 305- and 454-what nobody has made clear to me.)

Weather, summer weather, is what really separates urban and rural people. We are both on the same wavelength when it comes to wind and cold. Too much is too much. Snow should come on days when we do not need to go anywhere, and blizzards can be done without entirely. Country folk, though, have strict ideas about what constitutes good weather in the growing season. Dry for seeding, lots of rain in June and July, except for the days we want to summerfallow or spray, and bone dry from the middle of August until every bushel is in the bin. Doesn't sound like a lot to ask for, does it?

Once in a while I hear the weather people suggesting that a rainy weekend may be just what the farms need. If they keep that up, there may still be hope for compatibility. Of course, we will have to watch our vocabulary around them until they catch on to approaches, trash, dugouts, and such.

Counting on Tires

A FLAT TIRE ON THE COMBINE
PROMPTS A NEIGHBOURHOOD RECKONING

During harvest last fall, one of the big tires on the combine breathed its last. Luckily it happened only about half a mile from the house, instead of in the farthest corner of the farthest field, where most breakdowns occur. The tire service man from Moose Jaw was prompt and we were held up for only three or four hours, but the cost was over twelve hundred dollars. After the harvesters went back to work, I sat at the kitchen window watching them and thinking, "No wonder we are always broke."

I started counting up the number of tires that have to be kept inflated on our farm. Trucks, tractors, loaders, cultivators—there seemed no end. I quit counting after I got to 106. Too depressing. I didn't mention my musings when Jan and the men quit for the day and came in. I am convinced that talking about things like flat tires makes them happen, no matter how much wood is rapped.

Our neighbours, John and Lyla, were over the other night for coffee. The talk turned to tires. I commented idly, "We have more than one hundred tires that have to be kept inflated." That did it. Incredulous at first, they started to count theirs. Soon the math got confusing, so Lyla got a pen and paper to keep track. Their total was over 160 before they left.

Next morning Lyla phoned, saying that John was still counting tires. He was up to over 200; in fact, if he counted things like the tree planter and the building mover, which were seldom used, and older machinery that was still functional, he was up to 287. She had been speaking to a young neighbour, and had asked him if he knew how many tires he was keeping aired up. He answered jauntily, "Oh, about 50 I suppose." She suggested maybe he should count them. Of course Ev and I are recounting ours; our total is over the 140 mark now. It seems like I really started something.

Farmers spend the early spring checking their equipment for the busy days ahead. Batteries seem to be the big snag for us this year. Ev has been testing, charging, and recharging ours, and it looks as if we are going to have to replace a few. I counted the number of wet batteries that we have to use to start and keep everything going that has to go on our farm. After I got to twenty, I quit. I don't think I am going to mention it to anybody.

Wascana Lake, Regina, with the dome of the Saskatchewan
Legislature building in the background.

❧

And It Sets in the East

MENTAL MAPS CAN'T ALWAYS BE TRUSTED

There is a city in Saskatchewan that is proof that the prairie spirit defies nature itself. It has a little lake built into it, on a flat plain where even God did not see fit to put one. Stately trees line the boulevards, little forests grow in the parks, shrubs and flower beds delight—all this where sage, buck brush, short grass, and cactus were once the only plants tough enough to survive, never mind prosper. In this province where farmers spend days every year trying to get rid of stones, stone was imported to build our own little palace where the elected royalty hold sway. On these plains, where hailstones as big as golf balls arrive every summer, and the Regina Cyclone was only one of many, a glass-sheathed tower reaches for the clouds, twinkling blue defiance at the elements. Acres of the best farmland are being paved and cemented under every year to accommodate industrial sprawl. Regina is an anomaly.

Regina is also a nice place to live. There are lots of churches, schools, recreational facilities, and it is not a city where people have to equip themselves with double locks, mace, or guns to survive. True, there are neighbourhoods where it isn't advisable to stroll around after dark, and there are incidents of drug dealing, juvenile crime, and more serious offences, but Regina people still get horrified about this, and care enough to try to do something about it. Not for them the averted eye or stepping over the fallen.

Because Regina had only the railway to consider when the city was laid out, it is built mostly on the square. If your car makes four right turns, you get right back where you started from. After driving through Edinburgh, or Stockholm, or even Calgary, this is very comforting.

I take pride in my navigational skills. When we go south I do not have to orient the map so that the top is towards the north, and read it upside down. I can flip out directions such as "Turn left in two blocks," "This detour will put us on Highway 37 in four minutes," "That will be a one-way street, so we will have to go four blocks and then turn right three times," and "Take Exit B at the second intersection." I didn't even get lost in the West Edmonton Mall. I am good!

Except in Regina.

When I was seventeen, I arrived in Regina by train, after dark, and a taxi took me to my boarding place. The sky stayed cloudy for several days while I learned how to get to the secretarial school on Eleventh Avenue. In my mind, I had to walk north on Albert Street until I crossed the railroad through the main railway underpass, and then turn left on Eleventh Avenue to get to Scarth Street. Before the first sunny day, I had a map fixed firmly in my mind. It has stayed there ever since. It bothered me a bit that the sun rose in the west and set in the east, but that was the way it was. Intellectually, I realized that I was 180 degrees out, but I could not get my mental map turned around.

In those days when my map was being consolidated, my roommate and I walked all over Regina, to Darke Hall, to the old Eaton's on Broad Street, to church way out on Quebec Street, daytime or after dark, it mattered not. We knew where we were going, and never once did I need to know whether I was going south or west or whatever. We had the streetcar lights memorized and knew which ones to take when we felt rich enough to spend the fare—I think it was five cents at that time, but on our budget we usually walked— so I didn't even have to try to figure out why I would take a Dewdney North car when my whole being told me I was going south.

After I became more worldly wise, I looked back on those excursions and came to believe in guardian angels.

The year was 1944 and, because of the war, the city was full of all kinds of people: soldiers and airmen being trained, people from all over working in industry and service jobs, and the usual drifters and hangers-on that migrate to cities where they look for easy pickings. Not once were we approached in any untoward way, and not once did that possibility even cross our minds. Regina was a kind city even then, except for the winter wind. Portage and Main in Winnipeg didn't have a thing over the corner of Eleventh and Scarth.

In spite of my directional handicap, I still navigate for my husband when we have to go to Regina and get to specific places such as implement agencies or repair shops. He has learned never to ask me which direction to go, and I refrain from saying anything more specific than left and right. We only get tripped up by one-way streets and I refuse to take responsibility for them; they aren't even on my mental map. I think it is kind of neat though, that in this city that has defied nature throughout her history, for me at least, the sun sets in the east.

The aftermath of a tornado on the Comstock farm.

We'll Pay for It Later

WEATHER, TEMPTING FATE, AND
OTHER UNIVERSAL TRUTHS

We farmers are superstitious in many areas, although we prefer to call it pessimism, or even frugality. A while ago on the CBC, a meteorologist was discussing weather folklore, such as red skies at night, and whether fog means rain three months later. Weather is a life and death—or at least a prosperity and debt—matter to us farmers, so it's no surprise that we listened carefully. We aren't into predicting weather by the furriness of woolly bear caterpillars, or by how thick corn husks grow, or by the weight of a sheep's fleece (in fact, the nearest most of us in Saskatchewan ever come to a sheep is a roast leg of lamb or a cozy sweater). However, all conversation stops when the weather forecast comes on—not that we put much faith in it. I have even heard comments like "It is too bad they don't have a window to look out of."

To predict rain we rely on things like flies trying to get into the house, birds darting around near the ground, or cattle becoming uneasy and noisy. Apparently there is even scientific evidence for such things. Like many people, I can smell rain coming, although I can't really describe the smell. And the only useful thing about arthritis is that it predicts a change in the weather a couple of days early. My knees can't tell if it's better or worse weather coming, but they are pretty good on the timing. Winter storms are easy to foretell: a doctor or dentist appointment on the calendar will cause a blizzard. And calving brings on bitter cold—ask any cattleman.

The best way to avoid hailstorms, fire, or crop failure is to put on extra insurance. If you have it you won't need it; if you don't have it the Fates will take revenge. Never, never admit that the crop looks pretty good this year. This is the same rationale that caused primitive tribes to give their cherished children names like "garbage," "filthy rags," "stupid ape," and "rancid fat." No god would be tempted to steal anything so worthless.

When our kids were little they never got high fevers or earaches during the doctor's office hours, but seemed to wait until about eight thirty on a Saturday night. In the same vein, we truly believe that equipment breaks more easily on weekends or late in the day, after repair shops close. This belief explains the coffee-can fetish that is so prevalent among farmers. It used to be tobacco cans, but no matter what type they are, every farmer has a collection of cans that preserve: (a) an assortment of used bearings that aren't in great shape, but would serve in a pinch with a hypodermic injection of grease; (b) every size of bolt and nut in the world, except the one that breaks; and (c to z) O-rings, gaskets, points, spark plugs, cotter keys, washers, nails, tacks, rivets, and anything else small enough to fit into a coffee can.

There is stuff that won't fit into coffee cans that must be kept, too. Cultivator shovels are changed wholesale, but we keep the old ones just in case one breaks or gets too thin because it runs behind the tractor tire where the soil is harder. We replace a checked and cracked pulley belt, but string the old one on a hook somewhere in the shop. It might last until Monday morning if the new one breaks. A discarded truck tire will keep the disker going for a couple of days when the implement tire disintegrates. I have mentioned before how Ev wore a footpath over the hill to the junk pile retrieving bits and pieces he rashly hauled away when he got a sudden attack of "tidy." The rule is: "Anything that is trashed will be needed before many moons have passed."

As I say, I am not sure whether the principles and rules I have been talking about are superstitions or some exotic universal truths decreed eons ago by Destiny. I do know that I don't have nerve enough to defy them. We will just keep on putting on extra insurance, making alternative arrangements in case of storms, saving stuff, and continue bad-mouthing the crop until it is in the bin.

Most of us are neither millionaires nor paupers. Maybe that is because we take a lot of expert advice with a shake of salt. We know from long experience that there is no easy road to riches, and few of us have the nerve to try getting rich illegally, so we mostly mosey along doing the best we can with what we have. And just as a couple of beautiful weeks of weather in February usually means a really dirty storm in March, in the end we always pay for whatever we get.

Keith and Jan's wedding, 4 August 1979.
Apparently daughters-in-law also inherit "the look."

Hand-me-down

WHEN "HAND-ME-DOWNS" AREN'T JUST OLD CLOTHES

Some people think the phrase "hand-me-down" is a slighting term. I am not among them. To me "hand-me-downs" are links with our history, and include artifacts and attitudes as well as somebody else's old clothes. But let's not scorn the clothing, either. When we were kids my sisters and I always looked forward to Aunt Mary's visit. She was a pretty good aunt, but the big attraction was the box of our cousin's outgrown but good-as-new dresses that came with her. I was bereft when I became too tall to fit into them anymore. Occasionally a box of old clothes from somewhere down east came as "relief" in the hard times of the thirties. About the only thing I remember about that is that once our box contained two frilly, gauzy evening dresses, one blue, one green. Mom couldn't possibly remodel them into anything useful, but they sure came in handy when Carolie and I played "dress-up." We felt elegant, and would have even worn them to church if we had been allowed to. When we siblings started handing down our kids' clothes to the next cousins in size, I found out why these dressy "hand-me-downs" are usually in good shape. The only clothing my kids outgrew instead of wore out were church clothes, the garments they changed out of about two minutes after we got home, in favour of something they could horse around in.

Heirlooms are "hand-me-downs," too. I have a huge, fluted banana split dish, a relic of one grandmother's effort to enhance the family finances by opening a lunch room. It sits in the china cabinet beside another grandmother's cocoa set—a tall, iridescent, blue-green pot with a long slim spout, and six demitasse cups and saucers. Her son bought it for her with his first paycheque. Of course, it was too nice for her to use, so it was in perfect condition when we got it, and it will stay that way—it is too nice for us to use, either. We do have some useful heirlooms, an anvil made from a steel rail, a huge bread pan, dented now, but big enough for a twelve-loaf batch of bread dough, and I still keep sugar in an old tan and blue crock shaped like a barrel.

Less tangible "hand-me-downs" are sayings like "You would forget your head if it wasn't screwed on," and "If I have to stop the car, everybody in the back seat gets spanked," or "I am going to count to ten." My kids got them from me; I got them from my parents, and I am pretty sure they didn't invent them. They may sound harsh, but they work well. I occasionally braked, but never actually had to stop the car, and seldom had to count beyond five.

Females in our line have another useful "hand-me-down." It is "the look." A silent stare—menacing and tight-lipped—that can reduce unruly youngsters to a mass of quivering jelly, "the look" can replace hours of scolding and idle threats. My maternal grandmother raised eight children with it, and my mother used it in rural schoolrooms and on her five kids. My sisters and I all have mastered it and, at a recent family reunion, it was interesting to see that our daughters have inherited the skill.

Perhaps those who use the term "hand-me-downs" carelessly should reconsider, as it is extremely short-sighted to underestimate their value. Whether we inherit our grandmother's eyes, or our uncle's laugh, or Dad's .22 rifle, there is a precious link to the past. And as consolation for those who were never lucky enough to get a box of clothes, there is always the thrift shop.

Calamity Karen—"Now hold it right there,
you snake in the grass ... or I'll fill ya full of lead!"

Christmas Shopping

ALTHOUGH I LOVE THE SEASON, CHRISTMAS SHOPPING
IS NOT ONE OF MY "FAVOURITE THINGS"

There are some indestructible souls undaunted by thoughts of Christmas shopping. They enjoy it. At least in the world's immensely varied population, I suppose there must be people like that, but, I am not one of them.

I view most of the preparations for the holidays with a sense of pleasant anticipation, or at least satisfaction in accomplishing something that will not have to be redone for at least a year. This is more than can be said for laundry, mending, or tidying out the "everything" drawer.

The first step in shopping is easy—get a long piece of paper and write down the list of names. It's not necessarily what ends up as the complete list, but it isn't hard to write down, in categories, sons, daughters, in-laws, grandkids, and the sibling and spouse that it is our turn to give to this year. Grandkids are sorted by size and age. After a bit of thought I add some neighbour kids who call us Grandpa and Grandma, a good friend who helps me out through the year, and a few other people we especially want to remember.

Then we try to decide how generous we can be, taking into account the size of the crop, the price per bushel, and how many payments have to be made before the end of the year. Even that isn't too hard. Our grown-up kids will supply, upon request, a wish list ranging from the ridiculous (bath salts or a new Cadillac) to the sublime (something in our price range). Sisters and brothers aren't hard to choose for, we just get them something we'd like to get ourselves. No, it is the grandkids that have me buffaloed. For the older ones, clothes are absolutely out; anything I think is nice they wouldn't be caught dead in. Records, books, games, jewellery, cosmetics—the list of stuff where my taste and theirs vary wildly is endless. There isn't much use asking them, anything they really want they have already bought for themselves. And it's no use asking their parents. They are looking for ideas, too, and if they happen to think of the perfect gift, they aren't about to waste the idea on anybody else—no matter how much they owe us for all the trouble we took with them when they were little. Gratitude goes only so far. We will probably settle on a token trifle and a cheque.

Younger grandchildren should be easier to suit. Every year brings its "in" gift, like Tickle Me Elmo or whatever is the newest craze touted on television. My problem is that I resent paying forty dollars for something worth about ten dollars. I liked it much better when gifts like the "Genuine Lone Ranger Cap Gun and Holster"—now politically incorrect—were desirable toys, or cuddly, soft baby dolls that can't talk or wet, play pat-a-cake, or roller skate. A kid couldn't have too many pop guns, toy trucks, or dolls. I think that many popular toys nowadays end up being "spectator sports" and leave nothing to the imagination. There is little play value in them even before the string breaks or the batteries die. However, young kids usually have a list of "I Wants" a foot long, and I come to a compromise that I can live with.

The day finally arrives when the list is finished and we must venture into the mall or downtown stores to actually shop. We go early to avoid the crowd and find the crowd already there. Not a shopping cart is left in the usual rack, so I hover at the door and wait for them to be retrieved from the parking area. My list is at the ready, coat and purse in the bottom of the cart, as we methodically patrol up one aisle and down the next. "The Little Drummer Boy" and "Rudolph" assault my eardrums. I make two discoveries: first, most items on my list cost quite a bit more than I have allowed for; and second, the items that cost about what I thought they should cost are out of stock. All that is left in their place is the little price card and a bare hook.

Our list gets revised—practically all that is left of it is the column of names. From the expressions on the faces of my fellow shoppers, we are not alone in this particular boat. I keep wishing someone would step on the Drummer Boy, or at least on his drum. Several hours later we manoeuvre our loaded cart towards the lineups at the tills.

I am something of a Jonah. When we go to a buffet supper, people at my table have come to realize that it will be the last to be called to the food. When I select the shortest lineup at a bank, the little old man ahead of me will have three accounts that have to be searched back to July 1978. There is no use changing lines because I carry the curse with me. So, although we make a quick survey of the tills, I always manage to get into a queue where the clerk has to call the manager several times, the printing roll runs out, and someone's Visa card won't work. I have become reconciled to this. In fact if it doesn't happen, I have a superstitious premonition that something worse might—maybe I will fall and break my hip in the doorway, or someone will run into our van at the first intersection after we drive away.

We always manage to finish shopping, though. I quite enjoy the rest of the Christmas preparations—the decorating, baking, writing the Christmas letter, even making *lefse*, a thin, potato-based bread, which always takes more time to clean up after than it does to make. Despite the busyness, I also seem to be a bit brainwashed. Every once in a while as I bustle around, I find myself humming that rotten "Little Drummer Boy" song.

Grandma's Humbug Christmas.

Grandma's Humbug Christmas

When the days shorten up and the snowbanks get deep,
I wait for the hucksters' loud din:
"Only so many days, so shop till you drop!"
I'm dampened before I begin.

My Christmas card list gets longer each year,
And postage has gone through the ceiling.
But I greet our full mailbox, all eager to find
Out how old friends are faring and feeling.

The stores get so crowded, all parking slots full,
The stuff on my list can't be found.
My feet start to swell, yet I find I can smile
As I swivel my shopping cart round.

"Jingle Bells" blares from the shops down the street,
And the Drummer Boy makes my ears numb.
But old carol melodies cast their own spell.
I find myself starting to hum.

On the cupboard top dough-spotted recipes mingle
  With raisins and nuts and big dishes.
I bake in a frenzy; pots fill the sink,
  But the smell in the house is delicious.

With the best branches out and the worst side all hidden,
  The ornaments down from the shelf,
The fairy lights strung and branches hung bright,
  I am pleased with the tree and myself.

Wrapping the gifts takes Scotch tape and three hands.
  The paper's so flimsy and rippy.
But when ribbons are on and the tags firmly fixed,
  The pile 'neath the tree looks so pretty.

When Christmas Eve dawns there's a turkey to stuff.
  There's peeling and dicing and whipping.
I keep checking my list to make sure it's all done.
  (Lately my memory's slipping.)

The table gets set, and my clothing is changed.
  Cars pull up, disgorging the brood.
We sit down, say grace, and a young voice is heard,
  "Hey, Grandma, this lefse *is good!"*

Though winter winds blow and we're smothered in snow,
  And overshoes grow in the pile,
I find Christmas each year is a milepost of cheer
  That keeps life for this Grandma worthwhile.

Yes, it is that same 1929 Chev, minus the headlight.

The Window Check

It is so peaceful in the country, right? Well, farmers have to learn to be patient. There isn't much that can be done about the weather—snowdrifts in May, heat waves in early July searing a half-grown crop, and untimely rains that sprout the grain in the swath. We learn to take a bit of salt with the announcement of disaster aid that turns out to be more hot air than help. Anyone who works with farm animals—cattle, sheep, pigs, or whatever, knows that it isn't a matter of "I am the boss so you do what I say," but instead a matter of outsmarting them whenever possible, and fixing pens and fences when it isn't. A farmer may get an aura of power and control when he sits in his tractor or combine, circling the fields like a demi-god producing order out of chaos—until something goes wrong.

Obvious things like a broken belt, a weld that cracks, a missing cultivator shovel, or a tightly plugged feeder are taken as a matter of course and are fixed with no excessive heartburn. However, inanimate objects like machinery possess a perversity that is probably a gift from Satan. Farmers know this and are sensitive to anything that doesn't feel right. It doesn't have to be much—maybe an unusual whine, or a gauge that acts up, or a little thunk he hasn't heard before. It must be investigated and fixed before something major and expensive happens.

When a farmer pulls out of the field and heads back to the shop, a farmer's wife goes on red alert. It is possible to interpret the amount of frustration involved right from the kitchen window. When tools are being picked up and laid down quietly, it is okay to take a cup of coffee out and ask what is the matter, as long as she realizes she may be conscripted as assistant mechanic. Assistant mechanics hold bolts, run for tools, and pump brake pedals. No intelligence is required; moreover, bright suggestions are unwise and unwelcome.

If the view from the kitchen window includes wrenches being thrown down, arm-waving, or a hard hat flung the length of the yard, it is best not to interrupt. What is needed about then is a miracle, not an assistant mechanic. This is no time to mention phone calls, dripping faucets, or burnt cake. About the only acceptable emergency would be if the house were on fire, or labour pains five minutes apart.

Fortunately, a farmer's bad mood doesn't last long. Many years ago I heard occasional metallic clunks from the yard. From the kitchen window I saw Ev cranking and cranking our old '29 Chev. Every once in a while he would pull the crank out and whack the fender with it—and then go back to cranking again. When he finally came into the house he said, "I broke the headlight."

"Miss the fender?" I asked.

A smile crept across his face. "No," he replied, "I aimed at the headlight."

Birds

After spending my youth in school on a diet of Shelley, Shakespeare, and Keats, who all seemed to have a thing for birds, I was very disappointed when we finally got to the British Isles. Of course, by then some fifty years had passed since my school days, but even so! There were no nightingales, no skylarks, just a whole bunch of pigeons and crows. Maybe we didn't look in the right places.

I can't say the same for our farm; we have birds coming out of our ears. These days, our sparrows are feeling indignant. They stuck around all winter and think that they own the place. A dozen or so robins have taken to foraging in a group on the lawn, and the sparrows are flocking around, trying to harass them, but so far the robins are paying no attention.

We enjoy the birds, at least we enjoy most of them, most of the time. We have a lot of swallows that perform amazing aerial acrobatics when they are after mosquitoes. But, and there usually is a but, every spring we have to try to keep them from building their nests under the eaves. Their little mud nests are kind of cute, but we try to poke them down as soon as they are built. The swallows have a lot more perseverance than we do, however, and we won't destroy a nest once there are baby birds in it. So, for a couple of weeks every spring, I usually have a parent bird swooping past my head, clapping its wings with a menacing whump as it just skims my ear. Even the cats get demoralized for a while. I am not keen on the experience and it can reduce a young grandkid to a quiver. As well, baby swallows instinctively perch on the nest edge, head inward, when they feel the urge. It may keep the nest nice and clean, but long white streaks don't do a thing for the blue walls of our house.

Birds even influence field work. As much as we dread the devastation ducks and geese can work on swaths if the harvest is late, Ev will steer his equipment around any nest he sees when he is seeding. Summerfallowing brings flocks of seagulls who play leapfrog on the newly turned earth, gobbling up insects and scolding each other. At harvest time hawks betray their presence with shrill screams while they soar tirelessly above the trucks and combine. They are on the lookout for young rabbits, and the rabbits know it. They keep bouncing from under one swath to under the next, just ahead of the machinery.

Some birds are seasonal visitors. Goldfinches spend a couple of days eating us out of sunflower seeds, both spring and fall, and Bohemian waxwings clean the wizened berries off the cotoneaster hedge in March. Woodpeckers, juncos, and other birds that we see only once in a while send us to the bird book, to find out where they come from and where they are going.

As soon as the weather permits, we like to sit on the deck on the shady side of the house, to watch afternoon turning into evening. It's peaceful, but it certainly isn't quiet. The other residents of our habitat choose that time to assert their territorial claims. Meadowlarks, orioles, blackbirds, kingbirds, lark buntings, thrashers, and every other variety of feathered, winged creature nearby, flit through our trees or sit on the highest available perch, warbling, whistling, trilling and—sad to say, but I must admit it—even screeching. As the sun sets, their energy fades, and when shadows creep towards us, a different concert develops—spring peepers in the nearby pond carrying the treble while the bitterns (or as they are usually called, the slough pumps) kerwump out the base accompaniment.

We may not have exotic melodies like those of Shelley's "blithe skylark," but I enjoy our cheery yard full of birds, even if it is a bit noisy at times.

Unloading another hopper of grain, destined for the bin.

Thanksgiving

A TIME TO COUNT OUR BLESSINGS
AND GIVE THANKS FOR CANADA

It is good that we have a special time to take stock and count our blessings. Here on the farm, the crop was in the bin early this year. Two or three weeks of searing heat in July lowered the yield, but the grade is good and it is nice and dry, so we don't have to worry about rusty grain beetles. The kids were out to help harvest—sort of like old times for a week or so.

The garden stuff is all in, except for the turnips and I don't think I'll bother with them. They were behind the corn where the sprinkler didn't always reach them, and then flea beetles got at them before I realized it, so they are runty little things anyway. Our vegetable harvest was too much for us, so we gave some to the kids and took the rest to the food bank. The freezer is crowded with berries, crabapple juice, and ripe tomatoes to be made into jams, jelly, and tomato juice when I get around to it. I like making stuff, and it is nice to see the shelves full, but because I hate cleaning up afterwards I try to do everything in one great spurt, so there is only one mess to cope with.

The flower beds have just about had it by now; only a few brave petunias are left and some sturdy sedum for colour, but the trees and bushes are flaunting their fall wardrobe—yellow, rust, red, and orange. Summerfallowing is done, and most of the hay baling, too. We see big truck-loads of round bales heading here and there to keep cattle fed for the winter. I suppose we can be thankful that when the trees are bare we get a better view of the road.

I love to travel, but it is always so nice to come home to Canada, especially to the prairie, where you can see from horizon to horizon without forests or mountains getting in the way of the scenery. Canada made it through last winter's record cold and snow, and the disastrous floods of spring. This has always been "next year country" and the coming winter promises to be better.

It is nice that Canada is still in one piece and looks likely to stay that way. I think that we should be more thankful that we live where children are allowed to be young, where teenagers are allowed to dream and even to be unreasonable at times, where people can afford to become ill or aged, and where we rely on our neighbours more than on our bank account.

I am happy that Canada is so practical about Thanksgiving Day. Instead of celebrating on the last Thursday of November like our American cousins, we make it a Monday so that we get a long weekend out of the deal. Mostly I am thankful that it is early enough so that all that leftover turkey is just a memory before I have to start looking for another one for Christmas.

So once again, at the end of another harvest, my family and yours together will count our blessings and give thanks to our Maker.

❧

Manners and Mores

PONDERING THE GENERATION GAP

The year-round pile of shoes beside the entry door under-scores the difference between our offspring and us. I have not been able to figure out a way to avoid the winter-long pile of overshoes that grows under the porch washstand every year. Perhaps if we had only one pair each, that might be the solution. However, Saskatchewan weather determines the choice between stylish chilly boots, casual snug ones, or, when the thermometer is down and the wind is up, clunky Ski-Doo boots with felt liners. But in summer I do like to be able to see the porch linoleum.

Our farm home has to put up with us coming in with our work clothes, because we live here. About the only concessions we make are putting a throw over the chester-field for the after-dinner nap, and leaving mud, oil, and grease outside when possible. Leaving shoes on in the house doesn't upset me, but I find myself uncharitable when it comes to tractor hats. In our house, hats come off—especially at meal time. Even the pleas my grandsons make about having "hat heads" move me not an inch. I think it must have something to do with the generation gap I keep hearing about.

The generation gap shows up in what was expected of us, what we expected of our children, and today's more casual lifestyle. We were expected to eat at the second table when there were too many for one sitting, and if we were eating with grown-ups, to answer when spoken to, and otherwise hush up. Our children ate with us, or at an extra table if there were too many people for one, and took part in the conversation. Now the custom is to eat on trays in front of the television, with no discussion and very few opportunities to learn table manners or how to carry on a conversation. I wonder if it is an improvement?

There used to be work that children could do, work that was meaningful and necessary for the family's welfare. Things like washing dishes, dusting, carrying water and wood, caring for farm animals, ironing, and fetching and carrying tools at repair time—chores that even a kid could see were important. Not that we always enjoyed doing many of the things we had to do, but we did feel valued. Today's children live in a world of household conveniences that take over much of the drudge work, but also deny them any chore more significant than taking out the garbage. A kid can't work up much self-esteem on that.

I miss obedience. A friend of mine, who is principal of a public school, relates that when he told a teenage student to do some particular thing, the lad ignored him. After class he asked the student (whom he had penalized with a detention) why he had not obeyed. In an injured tone, the boy replied, "I intended to do what you said, but you only asked once. My mother always asks about five times." I can't say my kids were paragons of instant and cheerful compliance any more than I was, but we didn't have to argue with them, or cajole, or put up with insolence. I did quite a few "I'm going to count to ten" threats, but I didn't tell them (and really didn't know) what I would do if I ever got to ten. The kids never called me on it. I wonder at the patience of people who allow their little ones to act up, yell, and do whatever they please. I wonder, but I sure don't envy them.

Sin is another casualty of the generation gap. We used to have so many opportunities for little sins, like wearing too much rouge and lipstick, dancing, or smoking. (For women that is, apparently smoking was not as sinful if you were male.) These were pretty easy to renounce, at least temporarily, when you felt a bit of penance was in order.

They were a grey bunch of sins; black sins were things like murder, stealing, and almost anything to do with sex. We didn't have much trouble with most of the black sins—lack of nerve as well as lack of opportunity, I guess. Nowadays, society doesn't acknowledge either sin or sinners. There are just a lot of "poorly adjusted" people whom we must pity, and in the meantime we need to keep our insurance coverage up-to-date, our doors locked, and a can of pepper spray handy. I am afraid that bad taste is now considered more degenerate than crime, never mind sin! I suppose it is only a minor aggravation, but I wish that the section of the population who can think of only one four-letter word for adjective, verb, and noun, and use it loudly and often, would realize that it is in very poor taste.

The Mirror

My way is different, perhaps no better
                            But different.
I walk on tiptoe, being
            Diplomatic,
                    Tactful,
                            Obliging.
Smothering hurt with a smile.

It matters not,
                            My young resent
A comment shaped too quick, a question
            That intrudes without intention.

Resent, much as I did thirty years ago.

I look into the mirror and I see
My mother's grey eyes, looking back at me.

❧

Sometimes I Wonder

LIFE HOLDS MANY LITTLE MYSTERIES, LIKE WHERE DO
ALL THOSE STONES COME FROM EVERY SPRING?

The world is nowhere near as practical and common-sensible as it could be, in spite of scientists who do their best to interpret everything in the natural world, erudite commentators who take up the challenge of explaining political matters, and the rest of us who wander around just wondering why this, that, and the next thing.

A while ago Ev and I decided to go to Prairie Knights Casino, about forty miles south of Mandan, North Dakota, on Highway 1806. Mandan is not a large city, but it does have four exits from Interstate 94. We were supposed to take Exit 154, I think, and as all the exits before that had been to the right, we hugged the right lane. Of course it was the wrong lane, so we missed the exit and ended up downtown looking for signs for Highway 1806. We eventually found the sign, but were in the wrong lane again. When we finally made it through the underpass there were lots of street signs, but no highway sign for about seven miles. Now, I don't so much wonder why men will not stop and ask directions as why, oh why, do we women keep telling them to, when we know: (a) they aren't going to; (b) they get mad when we keep on nagging them; and (c) if they end up lost, it is not their fault anyway, because there should have been better signs.

There are lots of things I wonder about. Why are there so many stones to be picked from the field in spring—big ones? Do the ones that are too little to pick the previous year act as seed and develop in size under the snow? And if the methane that cows manufacture is such an important factor in global warming, why didn't the buffalo warm up the prairies for us a couple of centuries ago? I don't suppose their social niceties were any better than those of cows. We are told that about A.D. 1000 the Norsemen settled in Greenland, and the climate was warm enough then for them to grow grain and fodder. About four hundred years later a mini–ice age took over and settlements vanished. But how did it ever get warm enough to farm there in the first place?

There were no polluting industries, exhaust fumes from fossil fuels, or effluent from factories to blame for that greenhouse effect, were there?

We are told that each kind of animal and plant is a vital cog in maintaining the ecosystem and we should never allow any of them to become extinct. I wonder if that really includes mosquitoes. I think I would be willing to chance it. And now that it has been found that a little wine helps prevent heart attacks, a little coffee is good for arteries or something, and being a little chubby is healthier than dieting all the time, I wonder how long before scientists find out that a little smoking will prevent ingrown toenails or something.

I sometimes wonder about the way we use words. Even if what we say is exactly the opposite of what we intend, everybody knows what we mean. If someone says, "Don't forget to unthaw the turkey," nobody expects it to be put back into the freezer. When hatred, bigotry, and greed result in conflict in Ireland or the Middle East, why in the world is it referred to as a "religious war"? Why does "flammable" mean the same thing as "inflammable"? My computer occasionally asks me if I want to "replace" something, and I am not sure if that means it will put the same thing back in the same place, or put something else there instead. And of course the manual is not much help. How can a book, written by very intelligent people I am sure, sound and look so much like English and still be so baffling?

I wonder why society, which really means all of us, is willing to pay hockey players and bank managers, and others with interesting, clean jobs, such immense salaries, but think that people such as daycare workers who look after children and old infirm people, or cleaners, or farmers, or clerks aren't worth much. Which set could we get along without more easily? Why is it easier to get funds to explore Mars or to build bombers than it is to find money to feed the hungry and heal broken lives? Could it be that our priorities are off-kilter?

I wonder about those things, but I must say it is the little ironies that I spend more time pondering. Why can we not exchange energy levels with the toddler we tend? Why does washing the car bring on rain? Why does starting school change a child from a much-too-early riser into a slug-a-bed? Why can't we have a holiday to recover from one, because that is when we really need it? Why does nobody visit when the house is in perfect shape and the cookie canister full? We never lack for company otherwise. How do cats know which people really don't like cats, and why are they so determined to become intimate with these very people? Why can I never find a lost tool until just after I have bought its replacement?

It is not only me. Son Keith had a neat spray bottle attachment for the garden hose. It was ideal for applying fertilizer, insecticide, and such. One summer Saturday he needed it and looked high and low for it. He asked his kids and his wife about it. He inquired if someone had borrowed it, but his friends didn't have it, either. So he drove down to Canadian Tire to buy a new one. Finally, he got the spraying done and decided to put the handy little bottle up high on the shelf in the garage so he would know where it was next time. And he did—he set it right beside the one he had been looking for all morning. Yep, sometimes I wonder.

A spring-fed dugout in the Comstock pasture.

❧

Get Any Rain?

SOMETIMES SASKATCHEWAN WEATHER ISN'T ALL BAD

We are at the age when thoughts of retirement, even if unwelcome, creep into the mind every now and then. Until about four years ago, I occasionally thought that it might be nice to move to the coast, where winters are warmer, and flowers and trees don't have to struggle to survive, as they do here. It might be nice to live where watering plants didn't always involve hauling hoses and sprinklers around, and where the wind didn't beat everything to a frazzle.

About the middle of July that year I found out what living with a lot of rain involves. We got rain—badly needed rain, and I am too much the farmer to wish it away—but nearly five inches! After the third inch my husband walked from one window to the next and commented, "Well, they can turn it off any time now if they like." Not that he was complaining, just commenting.

The previous Saturday morning it had looked as if it might rain so I went out to the strawberry patch. I have old knees, so I sit between the rows to pick and it is much neater to sit on dry ground. After about fifteen minutes it started to spit, and Ev came out to see how things were going. When I said I was going to keep on picking, he grabbed an ice cream pail and started at the other end of the row. We got a bit damp before we were done. I had just changed out of my wet clothes when it started to pour . . . and pour . . . and pour. Lovely.

We farm hilly land. When I started to help seed after the kids grew up, I soon learned that uphill and downhill were not the problem. It was the side hills I had to compensate for. If unworked land sloped away from the machinery, the tractor had to make its path a bit onto the worked land or I wouldn't "fill the furrow." If it sloped towards the outfit, I had to allow for that by driving a bit wide. Because we have lots of sloughs and potholes, we seldom go a whole round without having to make extra curves. It does keep your neck limber looking back to make sure all the furrows are full.

Of course, the big advantage of our hilly land is that we never will be flooded out entirely. The sloughs and potholes may get a bit bigger, and we may get a few gullies if the downpour is too violent, but we have learned to live with that. We usually have enough trash in the soil to prevent much washing. (Unlike in the city, trash is good on the farm. It means that there is enough straw left anchored on the surface of the soil to prevent the wind and water from eroding it.)

By Sunday afternoon we had about three inches of water in the rain gauge. We went to a fiftieth wedding anniversary celebration in Moose Jaw, and it was easy to tell where the people at the party lived. The city people were saying "Isn't the weather awful," and the farmers were all going around with grins on their faces. I should qualify that; there were some city people who were appreciative, but they all happened to be ex-farmers.

And it kept on raining! I am not really superstitious, but I have this feeling that if I say anything like "I wish it would stop," it may never rain again, so I didn't. The rain gauge was nearly full by Monday evening. Sometime that night SomeBody turned the sky off and the sunshine returned the next morning.

The wheat was in shot blade (that is, just forming heads), so the timing of the downpour was perfect. About a week later everybody had to start summerfallowing again, so the fuel dealers were happy. With the morning sun working on evaporating all the moisture, we got afternoon showers every once in a while. Even the lawns and garden looked good—plants respond so much better to rain than to water from the well. Ev kept busy getting the summerfallow in shape, and I got lots of fresh air mowing the yards and pulling weeds. The path between the strawberries didn't dry out soon enough for the next picking, so I dug out my oldest slacks and running shoes and sat on the wet ground the next couple of times.

Anyway those three days pretty well cured me of any enthusiasm for living where it rains continually. Watching on television the devastation that floods cause for people who live on the flatlands really made me appreciate our hills. Now I thought, "If I could only find some reason to be happy about Saskatchewan wind!"

Within a week, I found the Saskatchewan wind to be a friend indeed. Hordes, crowds, multitudes, and throngs of mosquitoes appeared, and if it is true that only the female mosquito bites, they were 90 percent female. On windy days, the situation was tolerable; on calm days (and I truly didn't realize before that we had so many of them), I sprayed my socks, my slacks, a big shirt that I inherited from somebody, and donned my mosquito hat before I opened the back door. I never in my wildest imagination thought that I would ever wish for wind, but until nature took the little pests in hand and froze their stingers off, I was grateful for a stiff breeze.

You've heard of "barn bees," but a "shoe-shine bee"?

Things That Multiply

NOW YOU SEE IT; NOW YOU SEE MORE OF IT!

I have no problem watching magic shows. You know, where the guy in the tuxedo pulls out a forty-foot string of handkerchiefs from a ping-pong ball, or ends up with eighteen little rabbits popping out of his vest pocket. It doesn't surprise me in the least, because at our place many unusual things multiply. Mind you, they are mostly inanimate objects, unless you count cats and the voles under the snowbanks this last winter.

If they ever get over their fascination with sheep, scientists who are exploring the mysteries of cloning might be able to explain why things multiply. I am sure it is not an isolated phenomenon. It is the reason that no housekeeper ever has enough cupboards, nobody ever really finishes spring cleaning, and everybody's garden shed is full to the eaves, often to the point where the lawn mower, hoe, and all the other implements have to take their chances with the elements.

Take margarine tub lids, for example. A bottom drawer in my cupboard is devoted to the preservation of these useful little containers. I reuse the containers for freezing fruit, chunks of hamburger when it is on sale in bulk, and homemade soup or casseroles for quick meals in the busy season. Sometimes I use a couple of tubs for food scraps for the cats. When the stack of empties gets too high, I match them to their lids and take them downstairs to await berry or soup time. I am left with thirty-seven extra lids to throw out, so I am sure they breed and multiply when the drawer is closed.

Shoes have multiplied in our family ever since my mother started housekeeping. There are boxes and several closet floors filled with the things—and I don't even remember buying some of them. I realize that shoes have soles, but it seems that unlike the other kind of soul, no shoe ever gets beyond the hope of salvation. No matter how battered, leaky, outgrown, or just plain ugly they are, there is always the possibility of one more wear on a very muddy day, or the addition to the family of some really small person, or maybe my lower extremities might shrink. As for the boots with broken bottoms—maybe someone will need a leather tongue for a slingshot sometime.

Then there are pens. I admit to having bought a couple, including a black marker pen, and I have collected several courtesy pens from motels. But in no way am I responsible for that collection in the Velveeta cheese box in the top desk drawer. I even throw pens away. Every couple of years I get a "tidy" attack and go through the collection. Pens know when this is going to happen and every one coughs up enough ink to make a scribble, and is then tossed back into the box. There they sit and multiply when the drawer is closed. It seems that ink doesn't multiply as well, because when I'm in a hurry it is hard to find one with enough ink to finish a signature or jot down a telephone message.

I remove the labels from glass jars with good resealable tops. I like making jam, jelly, and pickles, and find these jars work fine for another couple of recycles. I give away a lot of jam and preserves, so things should just about even up, I would think, but somewhere down in the basement, when the lights are out, those jars multiply and fill my sealer shelves to overflowing.

Pill bottles, unmatched socks, gloves for the left hand, picture frames, baby aloe vera plants, buttons—the list could go on and on, and it isn't only in the house that this multiplication happens. On our farm, the last time I counted, there were vehicles and implements enough to need 127 inflated tires. Tires are expensive, but worn tires are danger-ous, and most of them are replaced before they are absolutely in shreds. There is a tire pecking order: those too unreliable for the truck may still work on the loader, or the harrow drawbar, so they go into the old granary. There is no good way of getting rid of tires, even the ones that are beyond recycling. If you put them on the junk pile and burn them, they send up all kinds of pollution and such a pillar of smoke that you will have the entire neighbourhood coming to help fight the fire. If you just leave them to rot undisturbed, they collect little puddles of rainwater for mosquitoes to breed in. So they stay in the granary and multiply.

We really don't need any magician to show us the tricks of multiplication. What I *could* use is one that is good at making things disappear.

Dear Sir: About Your Advertisement

WOULD I LIE TO YOU?

Last night we watched the same television ad repeated about twenty times. Some jerk had "helped" his wife put on a party by buying the wine, and was taking credit for the whole affair! The main response it evoked in me was a resolve never to buy that brand of wine. Advertisements will be, like the poor, always with us, but lately they seem to be louder, longer, and more infuriating. Some of them—a few—are cute. Who could resist "Give it to Mikey, he'll eat anything!" or the little girl who thought her teddy bear really drank the orange juice? Those are the exceptions to the rule, which seems to be that if advertisers can disgust enough people with scenes of personal afflictions, ailments, and/or filth, and put it on loud enough and often enough, they will be able to corner or invent a market for their product.

Oh, there always were some things that were touted as cures, even if the disease had to be invented. Remember "Pink Toothbrush!" and "Flaky Collar"? An affliction that "even your best friend won't tell you" was slyly hinted at by a foghorn that boomed "Beeee-Oooooh," but it could be cured with Lifebuoy. Note the nautical theme! Swollen toes on fire with "Athlete's Foot" could be quenched by Absorbine Jr. (I wonder what Absorbine Sr. cured.) In those days if anyone needed more intimate attention, they either had to decipher the clues in very small print or go to the doctor.

Two powdered laundry soaps had the main market. One had a jingle that repeated "Rinso White!" with a bob-white whistle that was kind of annoying, but if you were lucky you only heard it once a day. Oxydol depended on a cartoon strip in which two ladies walked in a back alley behind a yard where snowy linens billowed on the clothesline. A good-as-new scrub board sat in the garbage can, discarded, they found out, because "you don't need to scrub if you use Oxydol." I always imagined they met there again after dark, each intending to retrieve the scrub board, and embarrassed to pieces at being caught by the other one.

Ivory soap, which was 90-something percent pure (pure "what" they didn't say), in fact, so pure that it floated, caught on quickly. Actually, the manufacturing system went awry, and instead of gently mixing the ingredients, a bunch of air was beaten into the mixture. Somebody with a "Pollyanna" disposition turned adversity into advantage by highlighting the "soap that didn't get lost in the tub!" and it has floated ever since.

Mikey (who eats anything) had ancestors, the Campbell Soup twins, and they are still going strong today. They must be nearly ready for their old age pensions, but they have worn well. In the days before everything was packaged for eternity, there were cute "little drops of moisture" that lived in the only kind of cigarette pack that was then protected by cellophane. There they were safe from a demon with a red pitchfork who vainly sought to dry them out. Imaginative and entertaining!

In the back of comic books, there were two mainstay cartoon ads. One was for a "body building" course that featured a ninety-eight-pound weakling who was always getting sand kicked in his face. His Charles Atlas transformation not only increased his muscles, it also improved his features, gave him four inches in height, a better haircut, and a far more fashionable set of swim trunks! The other ad told kids how much money they could make easily, in only a couple of days, just by showing seeds or Christmas cards to their parents' friends and relatives. Everyone would appreciate them so much and buy them like crazy! I tried the Christmas cards. The first place I went with them, my relatives mixed up all the cards and envelopes (they were sets supposed to be sold at different prices), and only bought one card for ten cents. Mother finally bailed me out by buying the rest. She gave me just enough money to pay off the company, and I didn't make a cent.

My sister and I followed two quarter-hour serials on the radio. "Jack Armstrong, the All American Boy" offered to send us various prizes in return for Wheaties boxtops, but our unsympathetic parents kept feeding us oatmeal and cream of wheat, so we were out of luck there. We also listened to "Little Orphan Annie," who bravely fended off crooks and mean orphanage owners with the help of her dog, Sandy. In between locating Daddy Warbucks, who was forever going off to foreign parts, leaving Annie and her dog with unreliable people who kept losing them, Annie would send us a magic decoder ring and membership in a secret society in return for Ovaltine coupons. We did manage to convince our parents to buy Ovaltine, and we even drank it just to get the coupons. The ring was just a squashy tin thing, and we never did get called on to attend any secret meetings. It was a learning experience.

At least we didn't pester to get a device that, put in your mouth, would enable you to throw your voice, dumbfounding your parents and friends, or a fish tank that contained real live miniature mermen and mermaids, or the miracle plant that grew without soil, needed only watering, and could be planted on a bald doll's head.

On the whole, advertisements probably are more legitimate now, given the "truth in advertising" laws. All I ask for is more discretion, variety, and imagination. I really *don't* want to see itchy, sneezy, smelly, scabby problems, or the same ad repeated seven times in one hour, or be beaten over the head with sound and fury. In return I promise to: (a) remain faithful to favourite brands; (b) occasionally try the new improved whatever; (c) spend a lot of money; and (d) see the doctor when I itch, sneeze, or erupt. Come to think of it, that is what I do now! What could be fairer than that?

Me and the Traffic Police

TRUE CONFESSIONS ABOUT MY RUN-INS WITH THE LAW

I demoralize easily. I am sure that if I were ever tested on a lie detector machine, my pulse and respiration would run wild and I would probably confess to everything from arson to grand treason. Perhaps I suffer from a naturally over-active conscience, or have an unusual amount of original sin, or maybe I was taken to too many revival meetings when I was young.

I am really a very law-abiding character. In over fifty years of driving, I have had no accidents, and no tickets, not even a parking ticket. However, I have been stopped by the police twice.

Years ago, on a hot summer Sunday, my four-year-old and I were taking dinner to the men, who were harvesting a few miles away. There was little traffic, and Karen and I chatted and relaxed as we drove along. We were halfway through the deserted main street of Ardill when I noticed that the speedometer was registering a little over forty miles per hour instead of the prescribed twenty-five. I slowed down in a hurry. We had turned the next corner and were on the way up Gabel's hill when I saw, to my horror, the flashing light on top of a police car.

I felt my brain shift into high gear. I told myself, "Keep going slowly. Come to a safe approach. It is illegal to stop in the middle of the road."

Karen said, "What's the matter?"

I snarled at her, "I am being stopped by the police. Keep your mouth shut. I do not want to hear a word from you." I am not sure what vile secret I expected her to reveal.

The traffic officer checked my driver's licence, lights, and brakes, and sampled the gas tank to make sure I wasn't using purple gas. (At that time purple gas had less tax on it and was for farm use only.) Then he said, "Thank you," and started to walk away.

"Is that it?" I queried. He nodded. "Oh," I blurted out, "I thought you saw me going too fast through Ardill."

My next encounter with the police was about fifteen years ago, and I wasn't even driving. My sister had to go to the Mayo clinic for tests, and I was along for company. To get to Rochester, Minnesota, it is necessary to go through or around the twin cities of Minneapolis-St. Paul. The only city map we had was the little inset in the state map, so we fully intended to buy a good city map at a service station on the outskirts of the city. Unfortunately for us, there were no outskirts. Before we knew it we were on the east-west freeway—five and six lanes each way, full of traffic, and everybody driving like Jehu. I was too busy map-reading to see much of the scenery, trying to find some way off that would get us on the right road to the south. Anything I did find, we couldn't get onto because we weren't in the proper lane. We decided that we would just have to follow the traffic flow until we were out of the city, and then figure out how to get where we were supposed to be.

Suddenly a very long semi-trailer made a right turn just in front and to the right of us. Kay instinctively braked and swerved left a bit when she saw the semi's long tail swing into our path. Horns honked, but we didn't hear any metal scrunching or loud screaming. We had just started to breathe again when Kay said, "A police car is flashing his light at us. I guess we have to stop." I agreed weakly. About then, stopping sounded like a great idea.

After we stopped, a trooper lowered his stern face to the window. Before he had time to speak, I said, "Boy, are we ever glad to see you!" As we explained our predicament, his expression changed from indignation to sympathy, then to barely hidden amusement. He looked at our puny map, then went to his cruiser and got us a good city map. He gave us a courtesy ticket and explained several times the route we should follow. He kept looking at our faces and finally said "You aren't going to make it. Follow me." We did. He led us through miles of city streets and, when we got to the highway we needed, stopped and waved us on.

I certainly can't complain about bad treatment by the police, so far. Maybe my conscience is just doing its job. Anyway, no one will ever have to give me a lie detector test. If I ever break the law, I will probably run to the nearest uniform, babbling confessions all the way.

"We'll need a bigger shovel!"

Winter

YOU JUST NEVER GET USED TO IT

Today the sun is shining in the window so brightly that it is hard to write, but when I look outside, I see the wind is blowing last night's snow into our tunnels again. One would think after three score and then some years in Saskatchewan, a person would know what to expect. And I do—abnormal weather, that's what! I have lived through dust storms, hail storms, alkali storms, a couple of tornadoes, blizzards, and some heat waves that made me want to take off my skin and sit around in my bones. I have been frostbitten and sunburned on the same day. And do you know what? I'm still not used to it.

This year we had five blizzards before Christmas, starting in October. We took pictures of the front yard after the first one. It is a sheltered area and there were pillows of snow on the picnic table and benches; the evergreens looked like Christmas cards. That snow melted and we finished harvest. After the next blizzard, Ev had to shovel his way out the back door. Instead of cushions, the lawn furniture was topped with loaves of bread and a layer cake. We took more pictures. Ev opened our lane with his three-point-hitch snowplow.

We started wishing it would warm up to minus thirty degrees. We don't have livestock, so are spared the worry about feed and calving, but do have, or did have last fall, about a dozen cats. Ev put an insulated tarp on the old granary floor, laid a piece of plywood on sawhorses, installed a heat lamp, and covered the works with another tarp so the cats would be warm and cozy. Every morning he takes cat food, porridge, and water down for them. However, Old Mama Cat (mother, grandmother, and probably great-grandmother of the tribe) gets snorty every once in a while and chases the others out, so some of them are sporting frozen ears, and some are missing. I think human mothers who have spent the entire winter with kids underfoot probably know why she gets so owly.

So far we have had to augment Ev's snowplowing seven times by getting bigger plows to come in and clear the yard enough for us to get out to the road. We took even more pictures—in fact we have a video! Of course, every time the yard is plowed the snow has to go somewhere, so before the last little thaw the snowbanks were built up ten feet high in places. Right now, all we can see of the kids' playhouse is the peak of the roof, the merry-go-round has disappeared, and when the neighbour's kids were over the other day they sat on top of the steel pipe that the swings are fastened to.

Early one morning a couple of weeks ago, when it was minus forty degrees, Ev found the shop furnace had gone out. Unfortunately, it was only the lighting mechanism that had failed; the little pump that squirts oil into the burner was still working fine. The burner was full of fuel oil, and the casing outside the burner was well supplied, as was the floor for several feet around. Ev cleaned up the loose oil with the aid of a suction pump and all the rags he could find—a messy job that took a long time. He came to the house about three o'clock to warn me that he was going to try to light it again. He drove the snowplow tractor out first, in case he got more fire than he needed. Black smoke rolled out the chimney as the oil-soaked soot in the burner caught fire, and when the casing burned clean, black smoke rolled out the doors. Finally things got back to normal and Ev fixed the igniter. In the process his Ski-Doo suit and boots got so oil-soaked and sooty that he had to get new ones.

Then the house furnace started to make funny, roaring noises. It didn't do this all the time, just occasionally, like two thirty in the morning, or when we were watching *Jeopardy* or bathing. Ev took everything apart and fixed it, although he still doesn't know quite how he did that.

We had a dentist appointment in Moose Jaw one Tuesday in January. We had cancelled out the week before because of a blizzard. By Monday afternoon the forecast was for wind and snow, so we decided to go spend the night at a motel about a block from the dentist's office. It turned out to be a beautiful evening. We kept looking out the motel window for wind or snow—anything bad enough to justify spending fifty-six dollars to sleep in town. We were almost happy the next morning to find saucer-sized flakes of wet snow making the streets slushy and the wind starting up. We left town as soon as we were done and found our blizzard. We got as far as our gate before we got stuck. I stepped on a chunk of ice and fell down on the way up to the house. It is a good thing we didn't have far to go because the wind made walking up the rise to the house just about all I could take. The truck stayed in the gateway until the next day.

I hope the winter snow distribution people will soon take their holidays. A lot of our neighbours are in town for the winter, or on holidays where the weather is almost as bad as it is here. Do I sound desperate? The only consolation is that, being a farmer, I am sure that next year will be better. If anyone thinks differently, I don't want to hear about it!

Winter Survival

If we have to travel, we're set up for woe,
    (A phone call puts friends on alert.)
With shovels and snow tires, Ski-Doo suits and boots,
    A Thermos and lunch wouldn't hurt.
Scarves, socks, and sweaters are layered three deep.
    We really find travel quite nice.
Our prairie blood's thicker, we claim, and we know
    How to navigate snowbanks and ice.

The weather gets fiercer? The forecasts are grim?
    Dad warms up the snowplow in case
An emergency threatens. The lane could be plowed
    If we had the weather to face.
But snowbound is a word that seems worse than it is.
    If elements fury and rage,
With furnace and weatherstripped windows, we're set
    To ride out near any siege.

The freezer is full, there is time to bake buns,
  Or try out a new recipe,
Paint a new picture, quilt, or crochet,
  Unscramble the family tree.
Time starts to hang heavy? Dad's pacing the floor?
  The shop is still cozy and warm.
There always is something to busy him there,
  And lots to repair on the farm.

We count up our blessings. No mud in the porch,
  And not one mosquito to flail.
No mowing, no weeding, no flies, and no dust.
  No worry, no hoppers, no hail.
No army invades us. Elections are done.
  White frost rimes the windows and trees.
Our home won't get flooded. The earth doesn't quake.
  No spraying. No African bees!

The snowbanks get higher and broader.
  Dad shovels a path to the car.
We peer through the windows and shudder.
  Today's not the day to go far.
The wind howls at us in frustration.
  The thermostat's flipped up a bit.
With cocoa and popcorn, some books, the remote,
  We cozy up warm and just sit.

Las Vegas Hilton, 1997.

Vegas

THE PRAIRIE CHICKENS VISIT THE CASINOS

My but it's nice to be back in Saskatchewan again. After finishing harvest and generally getting things organized for winter, Ev and I treated ourselves to a trip to Las Vegas. Over two hundred prairie chickens from three provinces had the same idea, so six loaded buses left one cold, damp morning—correction, it wasn't quite morning. We left Moose Jaw in the dark.

A bus tour is not exactly rest and relaxation, you know. Up early—really early if breakfast is as important as it is to us. I do not function well until after the second cup of coffee, and Ev hates lineups, so we usually ate at about six o'clock in the morning. The first two days we made a lot of miles; Nevada is quite a distance from Saskatchewan. Our tour director, Corilea, kept us happy with games and interesting information about places we went through, and Dave, our driver, was cheerful and competent. We stopped for morning and afternoon coffee as well as for dinner, so we didn't quite get welded to the seats. On the road, every once in a while, Dave stopped the bus, got out and ran around to the back. Although it had just been replaced, some contraption kept loosening and made the bus lose power. Dave just wiggled some wires and away we went again.

Once we got into the mountains we saw five or six mountain sheep on a steep rocky ledge, and from then on no wildlife of any kind. Not a coyote, not a gopher, not a deer, not even a bird. There were miles and miles of sage and rabbit brush, and some cattle, although what they found to eat I don't know. Some of the valley floors were irrigated and looked quite lush, but there sure was a lot of territory that I'd hate to have to pay taxes on.

In Nevada we travelled through the Mohave Desert. The land became even more stark and barren. Native plants that prosper there are cholla cactus, a low grey feathery bush; yucca, which has stiff, lancelike leaves; and creosote bushes, which are so pungent that animals are said to avoid them. I can't vouch for that as I didn't see any animals. Farther south, a relative of the yucca appeared, the Joshua tree. Its gnarled, thick limbs seem to grope for the sky, each branch terminating in spiky olive green leaves. Because its roots use all the moisture around so nothing else can germinate, every plant stands alone in its own little yard of sand and gravel, as if spaced by a gardener.

Once in a while we could see, way off the road, a little flat-roofed shack, an old pickup truck, and rusted machinery beside a hole in the ground where somebody was trying his luck at mining. A more desolate life I cannot imagine.

And then: talc mines, Nellis Air Force Base (home of the Blue Angels and a place where UFO buffs claim to see lots of action), and soon Las Vegas, the city of lights. Dave took us all the way up the Strip. It had just turned dusk, so we got an eyeful of the extravagant light displays of a dozen or more casinos. Closer to downtown every block had sign after sign for bail bondsmen, pawnshops, divorce lawyers, and wedding chapels. We got to Fremont Street in time to see the light show. Whole blocks of the pedestrian mall are roofed by thousands of electronically controlled bulbs mounted on iron mesh. On the hour there is a light and sound show featuring egrets, butterflies, hula dancers, and whatnot, moving to music, and every few minutes a low swooping jet seems to scream down the street, drowning out all else. I gazed up, fascinated, until I found myself swaying and so dizzy that I staggered over to find a handhold.

Circus Circus, the casino hotel we were booked into, was typically immense. We were given a floor-plan map to orient ourselves. As well as four casino areas, there were jewellery and souvenir shops, restaurants, an amusement park, beauty salons, lunch bars, pizzerias, a raised area where trapeze artists, clowns, and acrobats performed, and more than three thousand hotel rooms. It took ten minutes of brisk walking to get from one end to another. For older or tired legs there was even a shuttle car on rails strung outside, high above the street traffic, to whisk us from one end to another. It was pretty confusing, and I developed a lot of empathy with one of our bus mates, who claimed he even got lost combining at night when the neighbours turned out the yard lights.

I had expected to see exotic people in Vegas—gangsters with suspicious bulges under their tuxedo jackets, dusky sirens in caftans, emirs with flowing robes, or maybe even a movie star in pearls and slink—but either they were well disguised or else Vegas is entirely populated by people who are just as ordinary as our bunch of prairie chickens. About the only time we got a little stunned was when a guard rolled past our slot machine, seated in a little golf cart that was pulling a trolley full of orange bags stuffed with money. His little train beeped along followed by guards wearing guns, and they all disappeared into a windowless room behind a locked steel door.

Canadians are a modest, retiring people. You can imagine the mixed emotions of my *very* Canadian husband when his nickel slot started to ring bells and play a very loud version of a Joplin rag. He had won two thousand nickels, enough to summon someone official to finish off the payout. He scooped out the first thousand coins. The bells kept ringing, the rag kept playing, but nobody official came. Other people came, stared, and asked questions— lots of people. The change lady came with her cart. She had to stay until the official came. The clamour kept on; more people came by, stopped and stared. I moved away a bit because my ears were getting numb. A semi-official came with a key, but he wasn't official enough to pay out the money, and the key didn't stop either the bells or the merry tune. More than half an hour later the official-enough official appeared, the change lady vanished, and we headed for the cashier with pots of nickels. I sure lost a lot of my affection for Scott Joplin's music that day.

It was a week of interesting ventures, good fellowship, and little sleep. We arrived home not much richer or poorer than we started out, and as far as I know, so did everyone else on our bus. I guess we can call that a successful gambling trip. And I have the perfect answer for anybody who says Saskatchewan is "miles and miles of nothing."

I will smile sweetly and say, "Just try Nevada."

❧

Las Vegas Bus Tour, 1997

We left before dawn in Saturday's chill,
    For nine days of sunshine and sin.
I'd been packed for a week, days crawled so slow,
    I was ready my fortune to win.

The bus seats filled up with old friends and new,
    Our gambling urge was afire.
We slowed up, pulled over, Dave left the wheel,
    And got out to wiggle some wire.

Past stubble and kochia, cattle and brush,
    Cross the line where our money deflated.
On to Butte and its mines, past sagebrush and sand,
    Corilea kept our spirits elated.

Dave kept wiggling wire, the trip was a blur
    Of lineups, restrooms and stiff knees.
Nevada at last—slots, cactus, and noise,
    Mountains and Joshua trees.

Vegas' extravagant lights and casinos,
  Exciting, confusing and wild,
Statues and fountains, ships, wheels, and slots
  Make Regina's casino look mild.

We leave mesquite, the palm trees, and cactus behind.
  None of us made enough to retire.
Then past gorges, mountains, and sagebrush again.
  Dave got out to wiggle some wire.

A tired bunch of friends, we look forward to home.
  I think I will sleep for a week.
We'll be ready to rally this time next year,
  To head south our fortune to seek.

꽃

Rural Politics

So, we are about to have another election. Farmers are in a quandary: do we go for a devil we know, or a devil we don't? I suspect, like most of the voting public, farmers vote "against" rather than "for." Not only against whoever happens to have just been in power, but against those whose platforms promise what isn't possible. We vote against things like promises of lower taxes and more spending, against tax breaks for the "haves" and further demolition of social safety nets for the "have-nots," against the indifference towards agriculture on the federal level. There is a tremendous cynicism about politics and politicians out here on the prairie.

It is not so much that we think that every politician is a crook—although we know from experience that politics offers splendid opportunities for crookedness. We are not lily white, and we have often been bought with our own money. Few farmers can refuse even a glaring bribe, because they know they will have to pay for it later, whether they take it or not.

We heartily resent the omnipotent claims of the obviously inept. We resent seeing our government eliminate subsidies according to world trade rules, while our competitors ignore them. We resent oil companies, manufacturers, and chemical and transportation corporations who constantly increase their prices and profits on our backs, while generous political donations ensure that no government will call them to account. We even resent the media for inflating political trivia and gossip into earth-shaking stories. How dumb do they think we are?

What would we like to see? That's easy to answer. We need federal support for our production similar to that for producers in other countries. We need education funded by income tax instead of by taxes on property, roads that don't shake our vehicles to pieces, health services available within a reasonable distance of our homes, and a government that realizes that if Saskatchewan agriculture goes down the drain, it won't be long before the rest of the Saskatchewan economy follows.

Oh, we will vote on 16 September, but we don't expect much improvement, no matter who wins. It would be nice to have more of a choice though—like fewer politicians and more straightforward statesmen.

On the Wrong Side of the Law

NATURE ISN'T ALWAYS KIND TO FARMERS AND SENIORS

First, let me assure you that I am a very law-abiding person. I always drive on the right side of the road, do up my seat belt, pay my taxes, and I still have the tab on our mattress that says "Do Not Remove." I have no problem with laws against theft or fraud, or even blasphemy. Well, sometimes when I hit my head on a corner of the cupboard door I might say something kind of—you know—but even then not in front of children! No, these are not the laws that concern me. It's the laws that govern the working of the universe that I find very irritating.

I don't mean the cute ones, either, like Murphy's law, where anything that can go wrong, will go wrong, or the Peter Principle, where people are advanced to the level of their incompetence. I mean the immutable, unsympathetic ones we all live under.

There is a law of diminishing returns. I'm not an economist, but I can give illustrations of this one. In its most simple form it explains why, when you write a three-page letter and send a cheque to your offspring, you will get back a note that says "Thanks." If you just send a letter, you will never hear about it again.

There is another example, which I must say—for reasons of tact, diplomacy, and family harmony—should not be taken to apply to myself. A woman can take note of the wishful thinking of her spouse throughout the year, and conspire to find out the exact make and model of some exotic tool or toy he has always wanted. Then she pussyfoots around so he doesn't see her buy it, and hides it until Christmas. Meanwhile, from the first of October on, she has been throwing hints like mad about how she likes sequined sweaters, or wondering why her watch keeps losing time. About 17 December he will confess that he hasn't any idea what to get her, and will she come shopping with him and pick something out. That is diminishing returns.

As far as the economic side of diminishing returns, I won't even get started on the subject, because as a farmer and a farmer's wife, I could keep on for hours, and I know that the subject has already been beaten to death. At least it might as well be dead for all the difference it makes.

Then there is the law of gravity. I realize that if we didn't have it, we would all scoot off the earth into outer space. I don't actually want to get rid of it; I just think that, as one gets into the "golden years," it could be applied less severely. It would be very nice for the more brittle-hipped, less agile of us to be allowed to fall and just bounce a bit. If the law of gravity would ease up a bit at the bottom of stairs and then resume at the top, it would conserve a lot of energy. The energy wouldn't be wasted because most of us use all we have anyway, but there are more constructive ways of using it than climbing stairs.

I suppose vanity comes into my resentment of this law, too. It has got to be gravity responsible for all the sagging. Just think how nice it would be if we didn't have to struggle with the sags behind and before, not to mention those firm rosy cheeks of youth that descend unnoticed until one day you look in the mirror and wonder where those jowls came from. I also just realized that being able to modify gravity at will would make it much more pleasant to get on the scales in the doctor's office, too.

The Law of Inertia says that a stationary object stays stationary unless energy is applied. The second part of this law is that once movement starts, it tends to continue. How true! How aggravating! Oh, I can get up and start moving if I have to. Mind you, since we don't have to get kids off on the school bus anymore, I find great pleasure in having two or three cups of coffee while still in my pyjamas. Of course, now that I have the chance, I can't sleep in anymore, but I have an easy chair in the kitchen, and I do love my coffee. However, if a car comes driving into the yard, I can be dressed, washed, and almost have the beds made before they get to the door.

The inertia part of getting started applies to jobs like painting the house. I have had scrapers, brushes, and ladders available for several years, and last spring I even got one of those slick paint rollers that doesn't need a tray, but fills itself with a trigger and a tube. I know the colours I want to use, the house really needs painting, and I could find the time. Inertia is really the only excuse I have.

I have a room in the basement that I loosely call my studio. It contains all the equipment I need for my ceramics and painting. There is even a work table in there, somewhere. There are also empty boxes, files, books, picture frames, pieces of Styrofoam, and unfinished projects, all waiting to be sorted, moved, finished, or discarded. That room is just full of inertia.

The no-stopping part of inertia also affects other kinds of work, for instance, vacuuming. I detest vacuuming. Once I have the vacuum out, a sort of mania takes over. The carpets, of course, are what bring on the vacuum attack. But once the beast is out of the closet, the chesterfields and chairs should be done, too. And the same dooey works for the drapes, so while they aren't bad, it wouldn't hurt to freshen them up. Shouldn't the mattresses be done, too? And while the beds are torn apart, I might as well do the pillows—oh, and the throw cushions. Are those cobwebs over there in the corner of the ceiling? While the step-stool is handy, I might as well do the light fixtures. Whoops, I nearly forgot to take out the floor registers and poke the hose down and wiggle it around a bit. There's probably crumbs down there. Speaking of crumbs, how about the bottom of the toaster, and the knives and forks drawer? Inertia!

I find mowing has the same effect on me. We live on a farm, so have a gas push-mower, a gas riding mower, and a whirligig thing that we call the whipper-snipper. The whipper-snipper needs an electric cord, a long one from the shop. The other machines have to be gassed up, and the gas can is usually empty. Fill the can, then the mowers, check the tires, the battery, and so on—well, you get the idea. Mowing is a major operation. If I work it right I usually get help. The riding mower handles the larger areas, and that is my territory, while my good husband push-mows out the edges, the corners, and the awkward places.

I start with the front lawn, move to the backyard, then mow the area around the garden. The big circle around the power pole comes next, then the driveway to the road, the old garden that has gone back to grass, in front of the granaries, out behind the trees—there is no end of mowable areas. There is just no good stopping place. In fact, if I didn't run out of gas (the tank only holds two gallons), I don't suppose I would stop before I got well out into the pasture. Inertia again.

I am not too sure I want to repeal the law of inertia, though. It gives me great satisfaction to have *done* the vacuuming, or the mowing, even if I am too pooped to appreciate it until the next day. As for painting the house, maybe sometime when the kids are home, I might ask them to do the high peaks for me. And maybe they won't find a good stopping place!

※

Perpetual Challenge: PC for Short

THE TRUTH ABOUT COMPUTERS

Richard Nixon declared, "I am not a crook"; I declare, "I am not a coward." After all, in my youth I was bucked or fell off a pony, several calves, and numerous pigs, and got right back on again. With much trepidation, I have hauled grain all the way to the elevators in Moose Jaw with a three-ton truck equipped with five gears and a two-speed axle, and I didn't break anything. I have faced numerous classrooms full of students as a substitute teacher, and went back again. But now—now I get scared every once in a while.

A few years ago my sons, who use computers in their work, talked me into getting one. I was doing four sets of books, and writing as well. They assured me that I *needed* a computer. It would be easier. The dealer who set it up for me here on the farm said, "Just play around with it— you can't hurt it!" So I played around with it, and it got hurt. A house call fixed it, but then it picked up a virus and crashed on 6 March. My son's computer did, too, on the same day, so we think it was from a game that my grandson had swapped with someone. So my computer went into the repair shop in Regina to be fixed and get more memory added. The boys kept giving me more software, updating me. They said it would be easier—not true. I became more faithful backing things up, which was a good thing, because the next year, on 6 March, it crashed again. More repairs, more updates, more software, virus exterminator, more money. Much easier, they said—still not true.

Then people started getting excited about Y2K. At midnight on New Year's Eve in the year 2000 the world may not come to an end, but millions of computers, including mine, probably would. Well, I am still scared of it, but I am more scared of being without it, so back to Regina: new computer, new printer, more power, more updates, more money, and more new software to learn.

I am resigned to not being fully computer literate, but I do like to think that I am print literate—until it comes to computer manuals. They look as if they are written in English, but really they are not. They remind me of the instructions that sometimes come with foreign imports with the warning "some assembly required." I recognize many of the words, but they do not mean what I expect them to. Even the questions that the computer asks me have me baffled. I am still not sure if "replace" means "put the same thing back in the same place" or "toss it out and put something else in there instead." And I deeply resent being told that I am doing something "illegal" when in my heart I know I am innocent.

Of course, by now my daughter is computering full steam ahead, too, especially on the Internet. A couple of months ago the kids told me I really *needed* to go on the Net. So I did, but I am leery of the chat lines. What I have seen of it is a little too raunchy for me. Also, I have learned not to click on every place it says to click. I like e-mail, although I still can't attach anything with any confidence that it is going to get anywhere. And anytime I get stuck, I e-mail one of the kids to tell me what to do. I hold them accountable for a lot of my anxiety, so I get even that way. I hope the kids have finished making things easier for me now. I am getting too old for this.

A Computer Owner's Lament

My enemy lives in a room down the hall
On a pedestal littered with paper,
While I read a manual, trying to glean
Some riposte to her latest caper.

She glowers—a sardonic leer on her face.
A message arrives but in vain.
"Error," she says, but I don't understand
What I've done to deserve her disdain.

I've given her backup and standby and even
Admitted I'm "Dummy," but yet
She won't give an inch. I'm starting to think
She deserves any virus she gets.

Then just when I'm ready to throw in the towel—
Revert back to pencil and pen,
Like a changeable child, she will act good as gold,
And capture my fancy again.

Sighs of Spring

SOME SIGNS OF SPRING ARE MORE
WELCOME THAN OTHERS

Well, March came in as lamblike as February had been. About the only evidence of snow seems to be a few ridges on the north-facing slope of ditches, a little mush under the trees, or in an occasional weather forecast. A few crows and a vanguard of geese are coming up from the south. Nothing much doing in the flower beds or garden yet, although I notice that the cats have been finding easier digging lately. Actually, I can wait another month or more for Nature to declare winter is over. The days aren't long enough yet.

Nature can wait, but other signs of spring come earlier every year. Spring and summer catalogues arrive in early December, along with the seed catalogues. Income tax preparers and RRSP sellers get their ads on display about the same time. Maybe they think that people are anxious to get at their tax forms. I think that it would be pleasant to be able to enjoy Valentine's Day, for instance, without being nagged about crabgrass on television. I suppose that nowadays one has to be a wee child to be allowed to revel in the pleasures of the present. As soon as one reaches the age where buying something—anything—is an option, the commercial world goes into attack mode.

One of the signs of spring I could do without is the "voice of doom." So far this year, in newspapers, on radio, and even on television, we farmers have been deluged with dire prophecies for the coming year. In fact, recently someone was looking ten years down the road, and guess what? He forecast disaster, too. This year we have been told that falling grain prices will keep on falling, prices that are up a bit will fall even more, rain will stop falling, grasshoppers and midges will do just fine, and new diseases are poised to pounce on all the alternative crops. Each announcement is just a little more sensational than the last. Of course there are the perennial irritants, the NAFTA challenges, freight rates, various politicians, and pressure groups. It is almost enough to finish off those of us who are still treading water.

I am a natural optimist and I live with a natural pessimist. We usually even out. I am happy all summer looking forward to a crop, while my husband is not overly disappointed if we don't get one, because he didn't expect it anyhow.

Between us, we have developed several ways to cope with the voices of doom. First, we remember that in the fifty-some years we have been farmers, we have yet to lose a crop in either March or April. Next, we read all the warnings and advice, especially those given out by the Department of Agriculture. Then we either ignore them or deliberately do the opposite. Either strategy works.

Spring on the Farm

The porch is a collage of mud and wet boots,
  The snow pants are mud-covered, too;
But the snowbanks are going, wee rivers run fast
  A'hurry to meet in the slough.

The yard needs a raking, there's trash to pick up,
  The bikes need a tune-up and shine;
But the tulips are poking their leaves through the ground,
  And the air is as heady as wine.

Gold stubble's grown dull, the trees are still bare.
  Shabby nests silhouette on the sky;
But the larks and the robins dart out on the lawn,
  And love is aglow in their eye.

Old raspberry canes must be gleaned from the patch,
  And the peony bushes raked clean;
But each morning I look for asparagus sprouts
  In the garden's dark promise of green.

The deer and the antelope moved to the hills.
Geese honk overhead in long vees.
New calves gambol awkward on pastures' new growth,
And crocuses stretch to the breeze.

Oh, our muscles will ache after winter's slow pace,
When each day brings a more urgent task;
But new life unfolds as the buds into leaves.
What more can a land-lover ask?

Dress-up day.

❧

Life in Reverse Gear

OLD AGE IS FINE, BUT SOMETIMES I WONDER
IF WE COULDN'T FIND A BETTER PLAN

I have written before praising the advantages of accumulating years. I am still quite happy about being a senior, and getting more senior every May. However, to be completely honest, there are some drawbacks.

I miss agility. I no longer have the urge to climb trees, play hopscotch, or zing round the bases for a home run, but it would be nice to stride through the world carefree instead of carefully. I especially miss my knees. I now pick peas, beans, strawberries, and weeds sitting between the rows, and leave a double row of indentations to mark my progress. They are not exactly the mark of my presence that I had intended leaving on the world.

I miss not having to wear glasses. Oh, I can still pick off a gopher with an open sight .22, once I locate it. However, the progression from single to bifocal to trifocal lenses does have disadvantages. It took about a month, the last time I got new lenses, to learn that the clumps of grass I walked over weren't fifteen inches tall, and I didn't have to step so high to miss them. And one does eventually learn that when going downstairs, there is still one more step to go when your glasses say you are already at the bottom.

I miss the guilt of sleeping in, and the rush of adrenalin that follows. Now I waken at five thirty and on my pilgrimage to the bathroom I gingerly move all the appendages, deciding just what hurts this morning. It would be fun to again snap out of deep slumber, half an hour late, and swish through the beginning of the day, bringing order out of chaos. I remember it felt just like being Wonder Woman, even if it only lasted a couple of hours.

I miss excess energy—sort of. I once started washing the kitchen walls and ceiling at nine in the evening because I had to wait up until eleven anyway for the baby's last bottle of the day. I don't want to do that again—ever—but it would be nice to think I could if I had to.

Maybe the whole aging bit would work better backwards. What if we started out old and got younger every year? We would probably come into the world bald, toothless, and drooling, but we now think babies are adorable in that condition. I am sure society would adjust. And then as we got sharper, and more agile and muscular—dare I say better looking, too—with each un-birthday, there would really be something to celebrate.

As we un-aged we could ease into the world of travel to exotic places, and even join the gypsy life of the RV set. It would be more carefree than it is in the present dispensation because we would not yet have developed the Puritan work ethic. Our consciences would never once chide us for wasting energy, money, and precious hours when we could be doing something useful. As the years rolled back, our bodies would become fitter, wrinkles would smooth out, and hair return to challenged scalps. We could take on more intriguing adventures, maybe skydiving, or exploring tropical reefs for sunken treasure.

As mature adults, we could look forward to having the children come home to visit. That way we could get used to them, and as our stamina improved year by year we would really look forward to having them around full-time. By the time they got back to being teenagers they would be finished with their wild-oat sowing and the general repudiation of adult mores and manners that kids usually go through in the process of becoming responsible citizens, so the stress levels would decrease from what they are now.

Young adults could look forward to university. Think how comforting it would be to graduate first, and then spend the next four or five years really enjoying oneself because the only requirement would be to become carefree, broke, and unemployable. As schoolchildren our lives would lose a lot of tension and frustration. I can envision children being praised for forgetting the capitals of South America, or how to do square roots or long division. And in the final year of school, instead of struggling with logarithms, vectors, and the dissection of pickled amphibians, there would be a year of stories, finger painting, Plasticine, and scribbling with rainbow marker pens, with naps thrown in for good measure.

Life as a toddler would be filled with increasing amounts of cosseting, rocking, and gooey appreciation for just being. Friends and relations would find immense satisfaction as we became balder, more toothless, and started to drool again.

I haven't got all the wrinkles out of the plan yet. As one who has given birth several times, I feel there has to be a better way than the logical next stage in the reversal. Maybe I will have to bring back the stork or the cabbage patch. I am still working on it.

Neighbours and family help out with the harvest, fall 1956.

Retirement

We country folk obey the law of the seasons.
With practised eye we scan the fields and sky.
Together we live through drought or hail,
Lend a hand when breakdown or illness strikes,
Rejoice when ripe grain's safely in the bin.

We criticize the government, curse the taxes,
Plow snow, pick each new crop of stones,
Tow each other's outfits from muddy holes,
Battle weeds and hoppers. We complain,
And yet would not be anyone, or anywhere
But who and where we are.

"A time for sowing, and a time for reaping," we've been promised.
We have watched each other's children grow,
Danced at their weddings,
Laughed with their joy,
Cried when they mourned.
Not quite family but closer than friends. Neighbours.

To reach the harvest of our years,
      Take things a little easy, let younger arms cope,
Means only that we've paid our dues.

Our eyes still keen enough that
      Through the masks the years have fixed on us
We see each other only ripened—rich and fruitful still.

"Seed time and harvest shall not fail."

✿

The Farmer in the Dell

A FARMER'S LIFE HOLDS MANY CHALLENGES,
BUT WE WOULDN'T WANT TO DO ANYTHING ELSE

First it was the farmer in the dell, and now it is the farmer in a mess. My goodness, we farmers must be either masochists or stupid beyond belief. The kids came home to help with harvest this year, so in between making meals and hauling out lunches, I had time to read and listen to woeful predictions about how we are going to the dogs. Everything agricultural is doom and gloom.

So far this year, we apparently have been wiped out or at least severely damaged by drought, too much rain, heat, excessive cold, midges, fusarium, railways, strikes, lockouts, grasshoppers, Europeans, low prices, Americans, high taxes, the Wheat Board, dual marketing, free marketers, and skyrocketing input prices. We should all be sitting around naked in the ash pile, scraping our boils with potsherds.

Somehow, we need to put things in perspective. Somebody is growing all that grain that the railways are charging too much to get to port, all the grain that plugs the elevators every other week or so. Somebody is raising the cattle and hogs that offend the noses of acreage owners. Those thousands of round bales from fields, sloughs, and roadsides that we see by the truckload are surely not just ornamental. Acres of gleaming new implements—combines, tractors, and cultivators—on lots at the city's edge are not just a dealer's idea of landscaping. Something has to be

The 1460 in action.

working right.

Saskatchewan agriculture has serious problems, true enough, but by turning every molehill into a mountain, the real ones are becoming trivialized. Let us not allow ourselves to be portrayed as victims all the time. Sympathy and understanding, which we aim for, can turn into pity and disdain when all the public hears about is calamity and catastrophe.

We have farmed fifty years now, and I suppose our experience is about average. We have gone through being dried out, rusted out, hoppered out, and hailed out. We once had several thousand bushels of grain in the bin and were unable to pay our power bill because there was no quota. There were years when serious illness or operations took their toll. Sometimes things looked very black. We are reasonably intelligent, so why are we still on the farm and intending to stay?

For some of us it is the challenge. With brawn and brain we wrestle nature, and man-made difficulties, too. There is satisfaction in using our skill to adapt and repair the machinery that multiplies our power. We bring life where there was none, plenty where there was little. We tend animals, watch new life as it is born, and sometimes help. We apply salve and powders, give shots to retain or restore health, and keep our charges clean and fed. In the evening we can see what has been done, and it is a little like knowing how God felt when He said, "It is good." When we win, we smile, and if we lose, there is always next year.

We produce food and clothing. No harm comes from our labour: no bombs, no wars, no lies or rumours, no addictions, no broken minds or bodies. We plant trees and flowers, try to make an island of peace for our families, shelter from the wind, and colour for the soul. And if we could, we would do the same for the world.

All this makes us sound like pretty noble and righteous people, doesn't it? To balance the account, I'll admit that most farmers farm because it is the best way of being one's own boss. We decide each day what the day will bring. We may work double hours in the busy season, but we can take time off without having to ask for it. It is easy to get used to. Ex-farmers probably don't make very happy employees.

My Estevan brother-in-law expressed the sentiment well. He is now farming after many years of working on the pipelines, and is occasionally asked to go back for special jobs. He said, "I have gotten so used to being my own boss, that when somebody tells me to do something, I feel like they are picking on me."

We farmers are a tough lot. We like what we do, and we will be here for a long time yet. We won't solve everything, but we have the ultimate weapon in our struggle with government, big business, nature, and the elements: Next Year.

Interior, Skara Brae.

A Child's Dream

A TRIP TO THE FAR-OFF ORKNEYS MAKES A
FIFTY-YEAR-OLD DREAM COME TRUE

One evening just after Christmas, our friend Roxanne had Ev and I over for supper. After we ate, I had a rousing game of Jenga with Owen, her nine-year-old son, which I won by a fluke. Then we four sat around the table and talked. The topic turned to Loch Ness and its monster. Owen enthusiastically explained facts and fancies about the beast and came up with a couple of ingenious plans for its capture, one of which involved a weighted net wide enough to span the loch and enough boat power to tow the net from one end to the other. How wonderful to be nine years old and have a dream!

I was nine and going to school at Boule Creek when I first heard about Skara Brae, a little Neolithic settlement in the Orkney Islands, off the north shore of Scotland. We kids often designed playhouses with a line of stones for walls, gaps for doors, flat stones for the tabletop and the stove, stones to sit on, and piles of grass for beds. The rules were strict: nobody could step over the walls, and you had to say "knock knock" at the gap and be invited in by the hostess. Skara Brae sounded like daydreams come true. I studied the picture of the little stone houses, made over five thousand years ago, and once upon a time lived in for real, by real people. I decided then that someday I would see it all for myself.

One Saturday, more than fifty years later, sister Carolie, friend Helen, and I drove our rented Granada north to the very edge of Scotland and got on the ferry to cross the Pentland Firth on our way to the Orkney Islands. Sunday morning we got on David Lee's tour bus. We visited an old click mill, which has a horizontal water wheel, then a pre-historic, round fortification called a broch. We also saw stromatolites millions of years old. (Stromatolites are fossil remains of a community of one-celled animals that lived on ancient shores when the world was young. They look like lumpy warts on the wave-washed rocks.) We visited the Ring of Brognar, a circle of huge monoliths about a quarter mile across, and went into Maes Howe, an artificial hill with a burial chamber inside that was made thousands of years ago. And we saw Skara Brae.

David stopped the tour bus beside a pasture and told us we had to walk three-quarters of a mile because, he said, "The useless government hasn't provided decent access to the Antiquity." He opened a bin at the back of the bus and distributed yellow waterproof pants and hooded jackets to any who would take them, as there was a fine rain and a sharp wind. I thought his outfits looked warmer than mine did, so I found a nice roomy one to put on. After I had walked a few hundred yards, the drawstring at the waist of my yellow overpants disintegrated. It was too late to do any-thing about it except clutch the pants with both hands and walk on.

We trailed along a rutted path in the tall grass. On the skyline to our left were grey stone buildings belonging to the Laird of Skara Brae. Just over the fence were fat, sleek, black cattle. None of them looked belligerent, which was comforting since I couldn't have outrun anything, espe-cially not while trying to keep my pants up.

Skara Brae was built about 3200 B.C. in a shallow valley about half a mile from the ocean. It had been occupied for around six hundred years when climate change lowered the ocean level. Sand from the bare ocean floor blew in and started to cover the site. When the job of keeping their houses out from under the dunes became impossible, the people moved on. Grass grew on the sand, sealing away

Skara Brae's secret. Several hundred years ago, the ocean started eating its way inland again, taking back its sand with wave and tide.

By the 1850s, the sea again reached the little settlement and revealed the traces of man-made walls. The Laird of Skara Brae at that time, who was an antiquarian (as were many of his class at that time), excavated four of the rooms. Then it just sat there until the 1920s, by which time archaeology had developed from the pot-hunting phase into a more scientific search for the secrets of the past. Skara Brae was formally excavated and became a National Heritage site, instead of a laird's hobby.

We walked on raised paths between the houses. It was like looking down into little Fred Flintstone doll houses. The builders had made walls of unmortared flat shale, all neatly fitted and about seven feet high. A typical house was about twelve by fourteen feet, with two or three corner alcoves leading into little cubbyholes. One nook was a latrine, complete with drain. The others were probably for storage. A stone-bordered hearth was in the centre of the room, and a dresser, constructed of long stone slabs supported with stone blocks at each end, looked for all the world like the bookshelves built with planks and bricks that many of us cobbled together in the lean years when we were first married. On each side of the dresser, little boxes made from thin slabs showed signs of being made watertight by mortar. "Baitboxes for live bait," someone said, but I think it more likely they were storage bins for seeds or grist, made to be insect-, rodent-, and moisture-proof. One side of the bed was up against the wall. Its headboard and footboard were stone slabs about four feet wide and nearly as high. The near side was a stone slab about fifteen inches high that would keep in a deep layer of bracken or straw to make a soft mattress. There were indications that the bed was covered on top and down the open side with a hide curtain, or some other fabric, to keep in the warmth. Several niches were built into the walls for storing the people's treasures. Grinding stones called querns, and other stones, maybe stools, lay around the hearth.

The roofs were probably tree trunks covered with sod or hides, as there is evidence that trees grew on Orkney at that time. Between the houses, except for tunnels to get in and out, these people are supposed to have deposited their rubbish, which sooner or later acted as insulation. I think it more likely that the space around the houses was banked with earth on purpose and the rubbish just got in there when the job was being done. I am convinced that these resourceful people were not stupid enough to shiver for years, with wind blowing through unmortared walls, until they had accumulated enough rubbish to keep themselves warm.

In the little office nearby we saw an unusual artifact: a four-inch, grey stone ball made from fine granite. It was carved into a many-faceted sphere with intricate designs on each face, and had a raised ridge around the centre. It must have taken months to make and if it was not an art object, I have not the slightest idea what it could be.

Too soon we had to walk back to the bus, me still clinging to my pants and warily eyeing the cows, who were eyeing me the same way. Even so my heart was singing, and I am not sure all the moisture on my cheeks came from the rain.

Maybe someday Owen *will* catch his Loch Ness monster. Dreams do come true. Dream on, little ones.

The Comstock family farm south of Moose Jaw,
with the Cactus Hills in the background.

About the Author

My father's family can be traced back to the 1500s in
Norway. They farmed the same land near Lake Mjosa until
the 1860s, when they immigrated to settle on farms in
Minnesota, and from there, in 1912, to Saskatchewan farms
on the prairie, south of Cadillac. Mother's paternal family
was given land in Scone, in the south of Sweden, by the
Swedish king as reward for their service in a war in the
early 1700s. They were considered "titled" members of
lesser nobility, but had to make ends meet by farming,
carriage-making, and becoming stewards of church property. Mom's maternal people lived in the north of Sweden,

near Lapland and Finland, and they fished, farmed, logged, and taught school. One of those old boys stole seven reindeer and fled to avoid prosecution, but returned home when Queen Christina declared an amnesty upon the birth of her son, about 1800. I guess what they say about every family tree containing horse thieves and kings is just about true.

I was the last child in the Kopperud family to be born at home on the farm, with my grandmother as midwife. Mother and Dad produced three more girls and a boy over the next eighteen years. I'm not sure we appreciated the humour when Mother claimed we represented five failed methods of birth control.

I went to school in a little white schoolhouse in Boule Creek. The community was noted for good softball teams, great Christmas concerts, and a new teacher nearly every year, because my dad, my uncles, and other young farmers kept marrying them. After taking Grades Nine and Ten by correspondence, I attended Cadillac High School. Those were happy days. I especially remember the high school plays, high jinks in the Chemistry lab, skating parties at the outdoor rink, and a special singing group of four or five of us who were often asked to perform at local functions.

Towards the end of World War II, I borrowed some money from my dad and took the two-month teacher-training summer course that had been set up to recruit warm bodies to fill teaching positions. My first teaching position was at Elm Springs, near Wood Mountain, with twenty-some children, including five who were taking Grades Nine and Ten by correspondence. I would like to be able to do that year over again, as I sure learned a lot about teaching at their expense. It's sort of like your first child—you should be allowed to throw it away after all the experimenting. After my second year of teaching at Welcome School north of Assiniboia, I took advantage of another summer term at Normal School (as teacher training was then called) and got a proper certificate. Mr. Fraser, my superintendent, and Mr. Andrews, the principal of

Normal School, recruited me for the job of taking Normal School students into my classroom for their practice teaching, at Mitchellton School. It was flattering to be chosen, but it was quite stressful, as there would be a visit from some inspector or another nearly every week. From there I was asked to serve as vice-principal at Limerick and then at Spring Valley.

When I taught at Mitchellton I met a young farmer, Evert Comstock. I mentioned that young farmers often found their wives-to-be teaching in the local school. Well, history repeated itself. Several years after we met, Evert and I were married on Friday, 14 January 1949, at my home country church. It was a beautiful sunny day, and neighbours had plowed snow for several days so everyone could get there. The wedding was at eleven, and Mom provided dinner for the whole works in the church basement.

Our first farming years included being dried out, rusted out, and grasshoppered out, so after my first son, Lyle, was born, I taught at Bishopric, a private school, to help out. Seven years later, another child, Keith, came along, and two years after that, a daughter, Karen. In that eleven-year period Ev had a stroke from an aneurism in his head, and a severe kidney infection; we bought more farmland—with a house that was bigger, warmer, and not as dilapidated as the one we first lived in; we planted more trees, remodelled buildings, and built a shop for Ev.

I kept busy mothering, 4-H-ing, helping with church and school activities, and later on started substitute teaching at Mossbank School. When the children grew up and moved out, and Ev's parents retired to Moose Jaw, I started actively helping with the farming and found it a lot more fun than housekeeping. Ev co-operated by pitching in with the house chores. By the time I hit fifty-five I decided if I was ever going to do all the fun things I wanted to, I had better start. I kind of thought that the world would stop turning when I quit the organizations and volunteer work, but it didn't. I took up ceramics, first just doing up greenware, but I soon turned to hand modelling, and also started oil painting

classes. I have this notion that I am capable of doing anything I really want to and probably overestimate my abil-
ity, but it is all fun, especially because I do not have to
try to make a living at it.

So far I have written up a lot of our family's history, a
cookbook for teens, some stories for children, and a
travel book, but the only writing that I have made any
money at are the humorous pieces that tell about things
as they were back in the good old days. Maybe that is
because, though I have very little creative imagination, I
do have an excellent memory.

My next birthday will be my seventy-fourth, and I am
looking forward to many, many more. There have to be
many more so that I can finish all the things I have
started and get started on a few more things I would still
like to try. Meanwhile, I still garden and keep up the yard,
help with harvest and other farming stuff like bleeding
brakes, fetching repairs, and holding things just so when
Ev is fixing them. We now have seven grandchildren to
keep track of, my siblings and our spouses have a bonding session at some resort or hotel where we eat
unwisely, talk a lot, compare memories, and enjoy each
other immensely.

Life is good. I've been blessed.

Update: The words you have just read were written by
my mother for her first book, *Aunt Mary in the Granary
and Other Prairie Stories*, or just "Aunt Mary" as we refer
to it. I can remember when the first copies of "Aunt Mary"
arrived in the mail, how incredibly excited and proud
Mom was of her accomplishment and we of her as well.

Oh, we weren't without our doubts, Mom included.
Would anyone buy it? Would anyone besides family and
friends be interested in the stories? Or would Fifth House
be saddled with a few thousand copies of a book gather-
ing dust in the warehouse?

Well, it didn't take long for us to see that "Aunt Mary"
was going to be a great success. Copies started to sell,

letters—"fan mail" no less—started to come in. If we were proud before, we had trouble buttoning our vests after that.

Mom was working on a second book by this time, *Sunny Side Up: Fond Memories of Prairie Life in the 1930s.* It, too, turned out to be a success and eventually, in the fall of 2000, Mom submitted a new collection of her stories for consideration as a third book.

Unfortunately, around that time Mom started to feel ill. Harvest of 2000 was a difficult time for all of us. Mom was frustrated, and even a bit angry, that she didn't feel well enough to help out as she always had. But we pulled together as a family and got the work done with smiles on our faces, even though each of us, I know, had secret fears about Mom's problem.

Just before Christmas 2000, Mom was diagnosed with cancer. She chose to postpone treatment until early in the New Year so as not to ruin the celebration, because, of course, she was confident she would meet this challenge and win as she had so often until then. Unfortunately, this was one challenge that Mom couldn't defeat. She died on 22 July 2001.

It is almost a year to the day of her death that I am writing this update for *No Spring Chicken: Thoughts on a Life Well Lived.* We knew that she would not have wanted this book to go unpublished just because she wasn't around to see it happen. So we've done it as sort of a labour of love in her remembrance and because her stories and books are an important part of her legacy. We miss her a lot.

Keith L. Comstock
July 2002